INDIE AUTHOR MAGAZINE

HELLO AND WELCOME!

I'm Indie Annie, and I'm thrilled you're reading this gorgeous full-color version of IAM. Did you know that you can also access all the information, education, and inspiration in our app? It's available on both the iOS App Store and Google Play. And for those that prefer to listen to me read articles, you can pop over to Spotify or our website. Happy Reading!

X

IndieAuthorMagazine.com

Download on the **App Store**

GET IT ON **Google Play**

Spotify

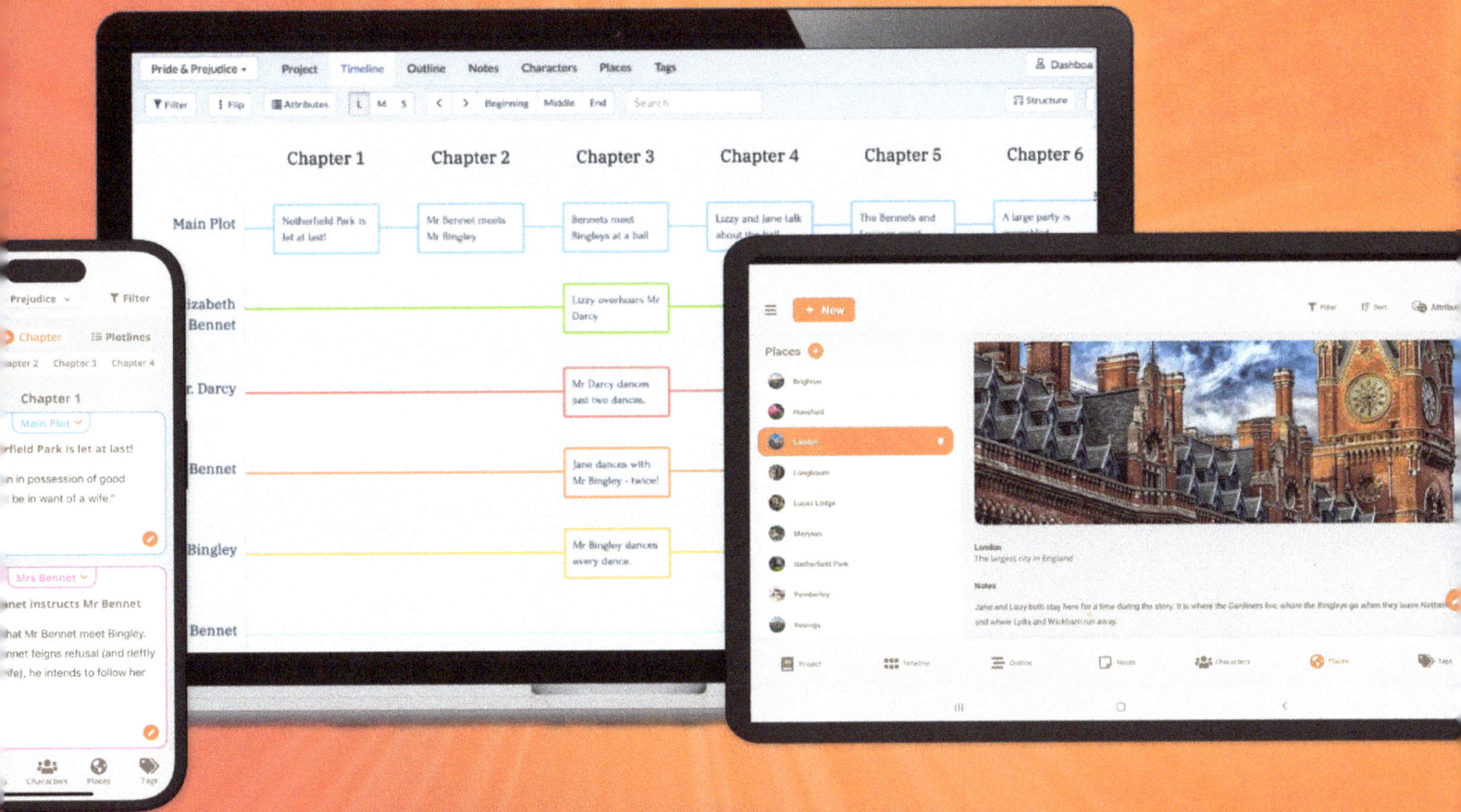

"I joined while having a crisis with Amazon KDP... The Alliance is a beacon of light. I recommend that all indie authors join...

Susan Marshall

"The Alliance is about standing together.

Joanna Penn

"It's the good stuff, all on one place.

Richard Wright

"ALLi has helped me in myriad ways: discounts on services, vetting providers, charting a course to sales success. But more than anything it's a community of friendly, knowledgeable, helpful people."

Beth Duke

See hundreds more testimonials at:
AllianceIndependentAuthors.org/testimonials

IAM

DISTRIBUTION

SO YOU WANT TO WRITE A BESTSELLER?

MARK DAWSON'S *SELF PUBLISHING FORMULA*

HOW TO WRITE A BEST SELLER

BUY NOW!

JOIN BESTSELLING AUTHOR, SUZY K QUINN, AS SHE REVEALS THE SECRETS BEHIND WRITING A CHART-TOPPING NOVEL.

Authorpreneurs in Action

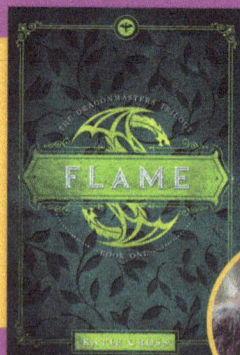

"I love Lulu! They've been a fantastic distributor of my paperbacks and an excellent partner as I dive into direct sales. They integrate so smoothly with my personal Shopify store, and their customer support has been top notch."

Katie Cross, katiecrossbooks.com

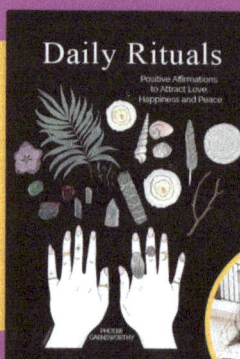

"Having my own store has given me the freedom to look at my creativity as a profitable business and lifelong career."

Phoebe Garnsworthy, phoebegarnsworthy.com

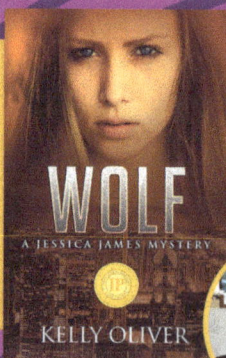

"Lulu has a super handy integration with Shopify. Lulu makes it so easy to sell paperbacks directly to readers."

Kelly Oliver, kellyoliverbooks.com

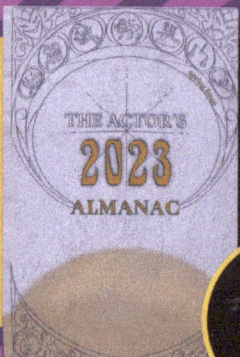

"My experience with Lulu Direct has been more convenient and simple than I anticipated or thought possible. I simply publish, take a step back and allow the well-oiled machine to run itself. Most grateful!"

Molly McGivern, theactorsalmanac.com

INDIE
AUTHOR MAGAZINE

EDITORIAL

Publisher | Chelle Honiker

Editor in Chief | Nicole Schroeder

Creative Director | Alice Briggs

ADVERTISING & MARKETING

Inquiries
Ads@AtheniaCreative.com

Information
https://IndieAuthorMagazine.com/
advertising/

CONTRIBUTORS

Angela Archer, Elaine Bateman, Patricia Carr, Bradley Charbonneau, Honorée Corder, Jackie Dana, Heather Clement Davis, Jamie Davis, Laurel Decher, Fatima Fayez, Gill Fernley, Greg Fishbone, Jen B. Green, Jac Harmon, Marion Hermannsen, Steve Higgs, Chrishaun Keller-Hanna, Kasia Lasinska, Monica Leonelle, Jenn Lessmann, Megan Linski-Fox, Craig Martelle, Angie Martin, Merri Maywether, Kevin McLaughlin, Lasairiona McMaster, Jenn Mitchell, Tanya Nellestein, Russell Nohelty, Susan Odev, Eryka Parker, Tiffany Robinson, Clare Sager, Joe Solari, Becca Syme, David Viergutz

SUBSCRIPTIONS
https://indieauthormagazine.com/subscribe/

HOW TO READ
https://indieauthormagazine.com/how-to-read/

WHEN WRITING MEANS BUSINESS
IndieAuthorMagazine.com

Athenia Creative | 6820 Apus Dr., Sparks, NV, 89436 USA | 775.298.1925

ISSN 2768-7880 (online)–ISSN 2768-7872 (print)

From the EDITOR IN CHIEF

Although you're reading this in January—or maybe even later into the new year—I'm writing this letter in December 2023. My family's Christmas tree is still halfway decorated. I still have packages to ship, letters to mail, and several deadlines to meet for our staff before I sign out for the holidays. I may be clinging desperately to the little time I have left this year to get everything done, but we are racing toward the end.

But on your side of the page, the end has come and gone. Instead of unfinished to-do lists or a mess of sticky note reminders, you're looking at a blank calendar and a freshly opened pack of pens, ready to take on 2024. While I'm looking at the final page in this book, you're already holding the next story in the series in your hands.

When you're in the thick of it, it can be hard to remember that every end is also a beginning for something new.

This past November, the indie author community saw the end of what had become a fixture in the industry for many: the 20Books Vegas conference spearheaded by 20BooksTo50K® co-founder Craig Martelle. But it was also the beginning of a new conference series led by the Author Nation consortium. In this month's issue, we share reflections from our community on what this end means for the industry, as well as what's known so far about what comes next.

As humans, we're bound to find endings worrisome or even a little sad—especially when what we're leaving behind is something meaningful. But as writers, endings are part of our job. And whether we choose to give our readers a happily-ever-after, a massive cliffhanger, or a bittersweet farewell, they can trust there's always a new story with countless possibilities waiting on the other side.

As I reach the end of this year and you stand on the precipice of the new one, let's make the next book in the series the best one yet.

Nicole Schroeder
Editor in Chief
Indie Author Magazine

Nicole Schroeder is a storyteller at heart. As the editor in chief of Indie Author Magazine, she brings nearly a decade of journalism and editorial experience to the publication, delighting in any opportunity to tell true stories and help others do the same. She holds a bachelor's degree from the Missouri School of Journalism and minors in English and Spanish. Her previous work includes editorial roles at local publications, and she's helped edit and produce numerous fiction and nonfiction books, including a Holocaust survivor's memoir, alongside independent publishers. Her own creative writing has been published in national literary magazines. When she's not at her writing desk, Nicole is usually in the saddle, cuddling her guinea pigs, or spending time with family. She loves any excuse to talk about Marvel movies and considers National Novel Writing Month its own holiday.

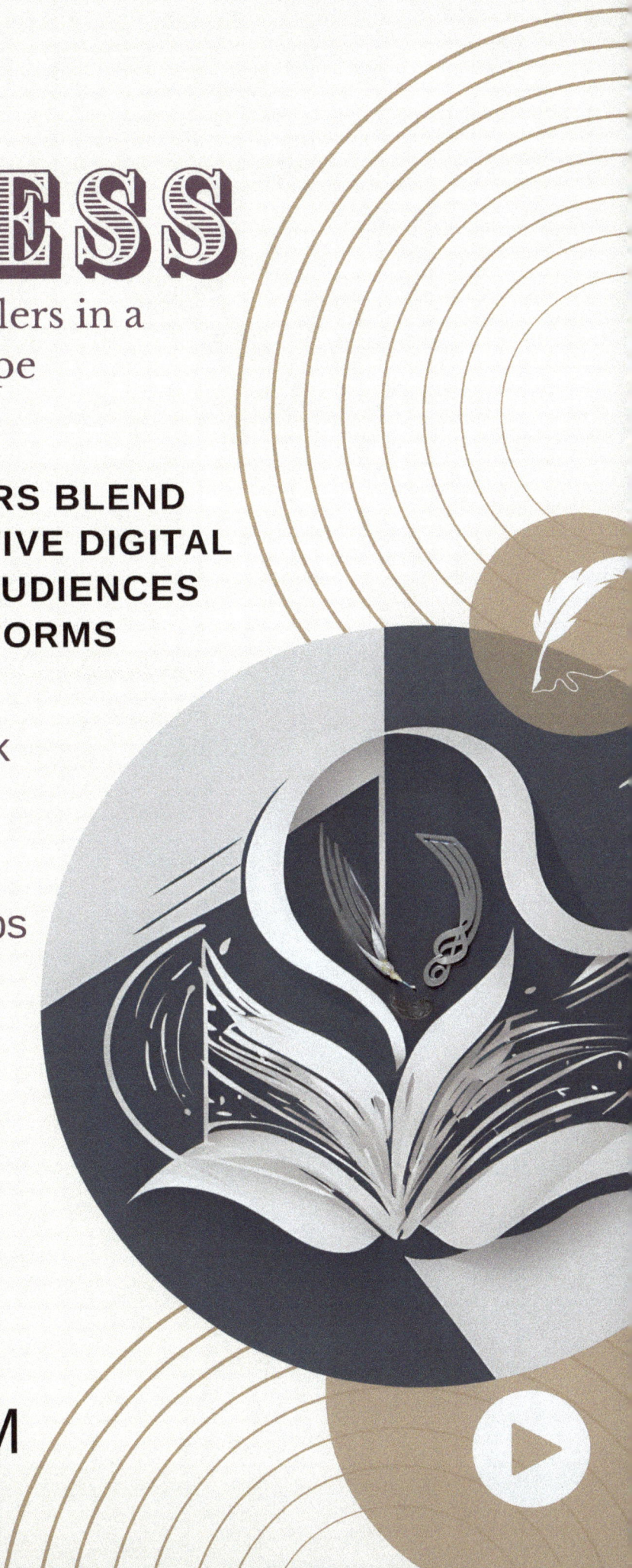

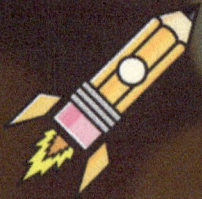

THE FUTURE OF PUBLISHING

A forward thinking,
exclusive conference
experience for authors
and small press publishers.

GET READY TO LOOK INTO THE FUTURE
HILTON RIVERSIDE NEW ORLEANS
FEBRUARY 26-29TH, 2024

futureofpublishingmastermind.com

Finding Joy (Not the Person but the Feeling)

An author career is a lesson in finding joy.

How many write because they aren't physically capable of other endeavors? It's the best of all worlds. You get to make money doing what you dream. It's an exceptional life, but not everyone makes it to the top. It's a mountain, and the path narrows as you climb higher.

Seeing people you started with go farther faster can be a mood killer. Seeing people who are new launch into the stratosphere from the start can make you question everything you're doing. Stop watching them except to learn what they've done right.

Your joy has nothing to do with them. You decide how you invest your time in the climb up the mountain of this fantastic career opportunity. Only you decide what you write. Only you can get better at writing and marketing. You are the only one in control of your joy.

I've known people with chronic pain and unimaginable trauma. They've been some of the nicest people I know. The creases around their young eyes tell the story of wincing with every effort. And yet they decide to make others happy by being kind.

As an author, you have chosen to share your thoughts with the world. Make your readers enjoy themselves. Make yourself smile. Someday, you could be someone's favorite author. That should make you happy. You may not be in control of a lot, but you can find joy in the little things. Finishing a book is such an occasion, even if that book is only a short story.

Celebrate your milestones, even if they're only inch-stones. Find joy in a career that doesn't take off instantly but is hard earned. If it were easy, anyone would do it. And not just anyone does it.

Maybe you're a glutton for punishment. Or maybe you're just committed, self-motivated, and diligent. You see what's possible: a career where you call the shots and get rewarded for calling the right shots.

It took me thirteen novels before I broke even. Nothing worth having is gotten easily. Take joy in your confidence that you will make it.

Peace, fellow humans. ∎

Craig Martelle

Craig Martelle

High school Valedictorian enlists in the Marine Corps under a guaranteed tank contract. An inauspicious start that was quickly superseded by excelling in language study. Contract waived, a year at the Defense Language Institute to learn Russian and off to keep my ears on the big red machine during the Soviet years. Earned a four-year degree in two years by majoring in Russian Language. My general staff. career included choice side gigs – UAE, Bahrain, Korea, Russia, and Ukraine.

Major Martelle. I retired from the Marines after a couple years at the embassy in Moscow working arms control issues.

Department of Homeland Security then law school next. I was working for a high-end consulting firm performing business diagnostics, business law, and leadership coaching. For the money they paid me, I was good with that. Just until I wasn't. Then I started writing.

Getting Your Book in Readers' Hands

"Distribution" may sound technical and far from the creativity of writing. But distribution simply comes down to how you can get a book from your hands into those of your readers as easily and widely as possible.

The Alliance of Independent Authors' (ALLi's) guiding policy for the most effective distribution plan is to be in as many formats as you can—e-book, print and audio—and in as many stores as you can, while making your own website the core of your bookselling operation for e-books and digital audiobooks, and increasingly for print too, as tools improve. As part of ALLi's seven processes of publishing, your distribution process must run smoothly for the customer purchasing experience to go well.

BEGINNERS

For new authors, the key to success is to achieve the widest possible distribution in the simplest possible way. Use Amazon for e-books and print-on-demand services to create paperbacks and hardbacks, then add an aggregator like Draft2Digital, PublishDrive, or StreetLib to take care of other e-book outlets through one dashboard and account. You can also add Ingram-Spark to the mix to ensure your print books are available for all bookshops to order, should they wish.

If you are at the stage of setting up your website, go directly to having a transactional site. Use a platform like WordPress together with WooCommerce, or set up a Shopify store, which you can integrate with your website. Selling your books directly to your readers makes your own website the core of your author business. ALLi's blog post from May 2020, "The Ultimate Guide to Selling Books on Your Author Website," can get you started.

It may be worth it to try joining Kindle Select, Amazon's Kindle Unlimited subscription service, whereby your e-books—but not print books—are exclusive to Amazon for a rolling ninety-day period in return for promotional perks on the platform. Some authors do very well in this program, but others do not. As royalties are calculated and paid by the number of pages read, poets or children's authors are unlikely to find it rewarding. However, because participation can be stopped after the initial ninety days, a new author could test whether their books do well, then decide to either stay exclusive or build Kindle Select into a longer-term business strategy—for example, running all new books through the program for a year and then going "wide," or non-exclusive. Overall, ALLi recommends going wide so that you have as many selling options available to you as possible and can minimize the risk of being reliant on any one platform.

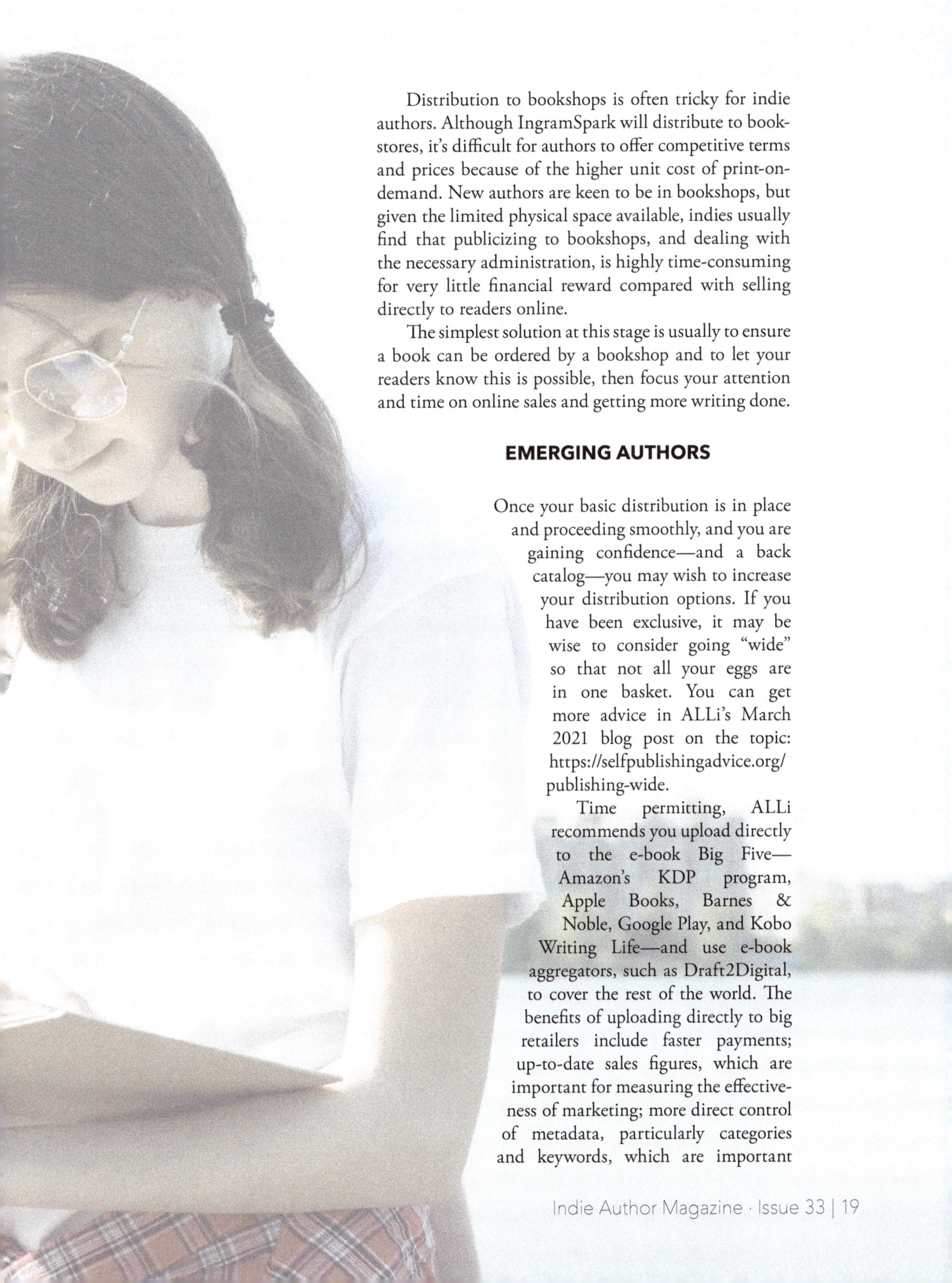

Distribution to bookshops is often tricky for indie authors. Although IngramSpark will distribute to bookstores, it's difficult for authors to offer competitive terms and prices because of the higher unit cost of print-on-demand. New authors are keen to be in bookshops, but given the limited physical space available, indies usually find that publicizing to bookshops, and dealing with the necessary administration, is highly time-consuming for very little financial reward compared with selling directly to readers online.

The simplest solution at this stage is usually to ensure a book can be ordered by a bookshop and to let your readers know this is possible, then focus your attention and time on online sales and getting more writing done.

EMERGING AUTHORS

Once your basic distribution is in place and proceeding smoothly, and you are gaining confidence—and a back catalog—you may wish to increase your distribution options. If you have been exclusive, it may be wise to consider going "wide" so that not all your eggs are in one basket. You can get more advice in ALLi's March 2021 blog post on the topic: https://selfpublishingadvice.org/publishing-wide.

Time permitting, ALLi recommends you upload directly to the e-book Big Five—Amazon's KDP program, Apple Books, Barnes & Noble, Google Play, and Kobo Writing Life—and use e-book aggregators, such as Draft2Digital, to cover the rest of the world. The benefits of uploading directly to big retailers include faster payments; up-to-date sales figures, which are important for measuring the effectiveness of marketing; more direct control of metadata, particularly categories and keywords, which are important for discoverability; and the ability to manipulate pricing quickly and easily, which is important for promotion.

A caveat: each of the e-book retailers has different dashboards and requirements, so going direct can be time-consuming, especially if you have multiple titles. Always consider the best approach for your own circumstances.

Another outlet to explore is libraries. Indie authors in the US can distribute their books to libraries via Draft-2Digital, and ALLi has a guidebook available—free to members and available for purchase to non-members—called *Opening Doors*, which has advice for getting into libraries, festivals, bookshops, and more.

EXPERIENCED AUTHORS

For experienced authors, now is probably a good time to consider expansion into bookshops, as you will be able to make the case for your titles to brick-and-mortar stores by showing strong and consistent book sales. This will entice booksellers to stock your work in meaningful quantities, either through your own logistics or via licensing print formats of your IP.

It is also the time to really increase your focus on selling direct as you grow a base of committed readers who are comfortable buying directly from you. This can include e-books, printed books, special editions, audio and companion books—e.g., workbooks— and premium special editions.

Not only will you make higher margins since you are cutting out the middleman, but you will also be able to access valuable customer data, including contact details and analytics, which again, by this stage, you are likely to be better able to put to use successfully. Read ALLi's "Ultimate Guide to Selling Print Books Direct" from May 2023: https://selfpublishingadvice. org/print-books-direct.

Distribution may not always seem a thrilling part of your writing and publishing efforts, but it facilitates your work finding its intended readers. A well-configured distribution system appropriate to your stage of business and personal circumstances can both free up a lot of your writing time and give your business important opportunities to expand.

Finally, it is important for all authors to review their distribution choices at least every couple of years. The self-publishing industry moves fast, and personal circumstances may also change. For example, if you find that you have more time or more admin assistance available, you may be willing to take on financially beneficial but more time-consuming options. New distribution options are always opening up and existing ones may change, so a business-minded author will always be open to revising their choices to make the most of their options.

ALLi has a comprehensive book, *Creative Self-Publishing*, free to ALLi members and for sale in our bookshop to non-members. Chapter 20 covers distribution. Additionally, ALLi has guides for authors looking to distribute books to bookstores (*Your Book in Bookstores: ALLi's Guide to Print Book Distribution for Authors*), and to libraries (*Your Book in Libraries Worldwide*), available at https://selfpublishingadvice.org/bookshop. ∎

Melissa Addey

Melissa Addey , ALLi's Campaigns Manager

The Alliance of IndependentAuthors(ALLi) is a global membership association for self-publishing authors. A non-profit, our mission is ethics and excellence in self-publishing. Everyone on our team is a working indie author and we offer advice and advocacy for self-publishing authors within the literary, publishing and creative industries around the world. www.allianceindependentauthors.org

Dear Indie Annie,

I really want to sell signed books, but I'm worried about shipping. The majority of my readers are in the US, but I am not. Would readers really be willing to pay extra shipping for signed books or special editions?

Multinational Merchant

Dear Multi,

Do you mind, my sweet, if I shorten your name? My darling, no need to get your knickers in a twist over shipping signed books abroad. You may struggle to believe this, my dear, but your readers will trot across fiery coals for your John Hancock. Just take a calming sip of Earl Grey—or whatever tipple takes your fancy—and I'll walk you through making that worldwide magic happen.

The first cardinal rule when wooing overseas fans: set clear expectations. Pop a cheerful banner in your online shop explaining extra transit time and charges for distant deliveries. Cryptic fees create crabby customers, but with realistic timelines and costs spelled out upfront, your loyal readers will take such charges in their stride.

Given lofty international postage costs, whatever side of the Atlantic or Pacific you are on, you could offer your badge-wearing bibliophiles incentives to make that hefty shipment worthwhile. Consider bundling several signed editions together to maximize each parcel. Who doesn't love a bargain? Dangle volume discounts and prize packs to entice fans to buy in bulk. Serial readers will snatch up sets of your sizzling or sassy tales. For prized items like limited editions, readers will also shell out

a few extra dollars, believe me! But do insure those precious parcels. Cough up the coins for tracking to ward off any wandering wonders.

Now if the dollar signs still make you wince, take command of production. Set up print-on-demand across the Atlantic through rapid publishers like IngramSpark or Lulu. Our tech-savvy modern book buyers are ridiculously patient for special editions. A few more days' wait to avoid steep duties? Most readers will understand.

The problem here, of course, is how to sign such copies. Here's where

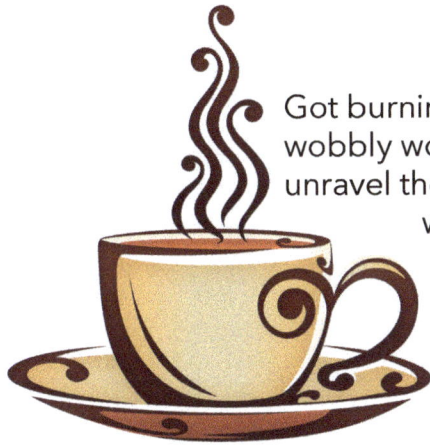

Got burning questions about the wibbly-wobbly world of indie authoring? Eager to unravel the mysteries of publishing, writing woes, or anything in between? Give your quizzical quills a whirl and shoot your musings over to indieannie@indieauthormagazine.com. Your inky quandaries are my cup of tea!

other authors have been creative. Try sending out signed nameplates. These are printed stickers marking the books as a limited edition you can sign back home in old Blighty, then post out to readers separately. Since you only need to worry about sending a small envelope instead of a packaged book, you'll save some money, and your reader will end up receiving two deliveries, each one sparking joy in their hearts. You could even take this opportunity to include a thank-you card and/or a small surprise gift like a branded bookmark.

Alternatively, you can manually order small batches and handle fulfillment stateside yourself. Just be sure to calculate all taxes and other extras. Niche mail carriers specializing in global literary logistics like AwesomeBooks can ease the journey. Let those postmasters shoulder currency conversions and customs declarations so you can focus on writing!

Finally, you could reach out to your fellow authors and see if there are writers in the US of A who need a base to distribute their volumes on the other side of the pond. This trade works best, of course, if you are heading stateside and they are planning a visit to your home country. When in town, sign your books, then wait for those magical orders.

I would caution you, dear Multi, to ensure that what your readers are spending extra for is worth the price and the effort. Can your

special editions include illustrations? How about gilded edges? Special edition short stories available nowhere else? Colored pages? If your world is unique, consider commissioning a map. Maybe even a treasure hunt? Put a secret code on the back page that readers can use on your website to unlock a host of other goodies.

Most critically, don't fret about fussing your fans with shipping times and costs. They'll feel downright chuffed at those personal touches making the long voyage from your world to theirs!

Remember, dear heart, that your fans love your books. Casual readers might be happy with a digital copy, and some will donate their print copies to the local library when they have finished. But your true fans, those who will cherish your autograph and snap up your limited editions, are prepared to wait and to pay a higher price. Now off you go to pack those boxes, darling. Keep calm and carry on connecting with your community across the pond!

Happy writing,
Indie Annie
X

10 TIPS FOR
AUTHOR EVENTS ON DISCORD

Ever wanted to find a single virtual space where readers could chat, you could give presentations, and you could hold online book launches or other events? Welcome to Discord! Discord is a place of many "servers," or communities. Each one offers threaded text conversation and the ability to talk in real time to people via webcam and microphone. You exist there as an "avatar," which has an image you choose and the ability to list a short bio and links of your choosing.

My introduction to Discord was during the pandemic. All of my in-person venues shut down, and I had nowhere to sell my books or do readings. I learned one of the larger Science Fiction conventions in the states was attempting to go virtual for the first time. The backbone of their system was Discord. The experiment was a hit, and most conventions and conferences followed their format for many years. There are still many online conferences that use Discord as their primary meeting place for networking.

As an indie author, you might wonder if the platform is worth the time to cultivate, but there are plenty of opportunities and creative ways to make the platform useful to your author business. *IAM* has covered the platform in the past, but if you're interested in exploring Discord's abilities as an events space, read on for ten tips to making the most of the experience.

FOR DISCORD USERS WHO DON'T OWN A SERVER:

(1) SET UP A FREE ACCOUNT TO ACCESS SERVERS
Discord comes in two flavors: the free version and Nitro, which is around $10 a month. Paying for the service gives you more bells and whistles, such as extra emoji; the ability to use a different avatar, profile theme, banner and bio in each of your servers; and more. However, the free version is also robust. You can host your own server on a free plan and network as a professional writer.

Pro Tip: Your Avatar's note section is a powerful tool for connecting with others in a Discord server. Users have a limited number of characters available to display their contact information, but consider posting a single URL landing page—I use a free service called LinkTree (https://linktr.ee/)—along with a tagline for your author brand. This allows potential readers and fellow writers to find your website, books, and contact information outside of Discord. It is a virtual version of a business card.

② PARTICIPATE IN VIRTUAL CONFERENCES

With a Discord account, you can apply to be a virtual panelist or speaker at an online conference or convention in your genre. These conventions and conferences have become established over the past few years on Discord and often return annually.

You not only will be seen by potential readers, but it also will allow you to build expertise as a speaker. Even if virtual panels are presented on YouTube or a private video streaming service, you can still network at these events on Discord, with no need for a server of your own.

---

③ SELL AUTHOR MERCH AND BOOKS AS A CONVENTION VENDOR

If you have not set up your own server or only have a small one, a good way to meet with potential readers and grow your own server is to join a larger virtual convention as an author vendor or small press. These Discord-based conventions will often create a section of channels for their "vendors" and assign a channel to you. Some will also feature you on their website. During the convention, you can run content on your channel, much like a Facebook or Instagram party. It is possible to be a speaker and panelist and still host an "author table" at the same time. If you would rather do a simple reading and no more, hosting a merch channel might be the way to sell your books at these larger events.

Pro Tip: You need to have an online point of sale set up with your books, such as Shopify (https://www.shopify.com/) or Etsy (https://www.etsy.com/), to distribute merchandise at online conventions like these. This online shop needs to be set up well ahead of the event, but while this takes time, once the shop is ready, it is only a matter of upkeep for future Discord events.

FOR DISCORD USERS WHO OWN A SERVER:

④ CREATE YOUR OWN SERVER FOR YOUR READERS

If you're looking for a way to connect with your current readers and grow your audience, consider setting up your own Discord server. Setting up your own server is free, but there is a learning curve. A Discord server is an enclosed community of chat channels with the addition of video and voice channels.

Creating channels can be a balancing act; some owners put in too many, so their readers get lost and discouraged as they wander empty threads, and some put in too few, making their server seem to be not worth the time. Consider the following text channels for your server, though it may be best to limit yourself to only one voice or video channel initially so as not to create overwhelm:

- a welcome channel for newcomers,
- an admin channel for you and moderators to chat in private,
- a channel where newcomers can set their roles, and
- a general topic channel.

It is possible to set up your server so that newcomers don't have access to the regular chat and voice channels until they have set their "roles" and been approved by a moderator. This practice helps to prevent spammers or trolls from entering your space and causing disruptions. A role is a tag moderators place on users. These tags could be as simple as the user's pronouns, what genre they write, or what country the person is from.

Bots can also serve many purposes—for example, user onboarding, running automated scripts to add features to your server, or management tasks. Select a Discord bot from a website such as Top Discord Bots & Discord Apps (top.gg). Click on "Invite" on the bot website. Select your server, and grant the bot the permissions it needs. The bot will then be added to your Discord server.

Pro Tip: Using Discord as a perk for a Patreon (https://www.patreon.com/) or Ko-Fi (https://ko-fi.com) account is a good way to build your reader community and allow your Discord server to make income. Manage your server with bots, and use Patreon or Ko-Fi to automate the onboarding process to your server.

5 HOST WRITING SPRINTS OR CO-WRITING SESSIONS

Your Discord server can be a great place to connect with fellow authors. Set up dedicated channels for writing sprints to boost productivity and create a sense of community among fellow writers. There are automated bots to do the timing for you, but holding sprints with a human host seems to be more of a draw.

Similar to writing sprints, a co-writing session is when a group of writers gather and work on their books together. It should be a mix of networking and conversation for a few minutes followed by a quiet period of intense work and could be a great way to utilize the video/microphone channels. Use a combination of Discord and your subscription service to announce the writing dates.

The choice to host voice or video events on Discord is a matter of audience size. If your groups are smaller than six people, keeping the session inside of Discord should be effective and less expensive. If groups are larger, Discord may not have the bandwidth to handle all the people, and it might be prudent to move the co-writing to Zoom or a similar video meeting software system.

6 BUILD EXCITEMENT FOR NEW RELEASES WITH VIRTUAL EVENTS

Build anticipation for your upcoming book releases by organizing cover reveals and other promotional events on your Discord server. This is a good time to provide exclusive sneak peeks, behind-the-scenes content, or bonus material to your members as a reward for their support. You could post your cover on channels or offer it as a file on your server.

To prepare for the event, publicize when your readers need to be on the server. Plan to host a talk about your new book to those who attend on a video channel just as you would in a real-world space. Have digital freebies to give to attendees.

7 LAUNCH YOUR BOOKS ON YOUR DISCORD SERVER

After building anticipation for upcoming books via cover reveals, host a virtual launch party on Discord when your books release. You can interact with readers, answer questions, and celebrate your book. Similar to a Facebook or Instagram party, you can invite your readers to join you during the launch and schedule live Q&A sessions where readers can ask you questions directly.

8 BOOST READER ENGAGEMENT

Create channels on your server for your readers to discuss your books, share fan art, and connect with one another. Separate each topic into a different channel to help people understand where to post their comments. Use Discord as a platform to build a supportive and engaged community around your work and foster a sense of belonging among your readers.

9   SET UP A FILE REPOSITORY

You can set up a "one-person server" to store manuscript files in Discord. The platform offers plenty of storage space with both the free and Nitro accounts, and it gives the owner a place in the cloud to access their work.

On a community server, any owner or moderator can set files as downloadable to users. Authors could upload downloadable excerpts of future work, digital prints of covers or characters, or other freebies you may wish to offer to your readers.

You could use Discord as a host for beta readers. Load your ARCs into the Files repository, and set up Google Forms for the readers to fill out once they've read your book. The entire system would be contained on the server, and your beta readers, coming from your fanbase, would find the task to be great fun.

---

10   USE DISCORD TO PROMOTE YOUR OTHER SOCIALS

Remember to post links to your other social platforms within Discord. For instance, if you have a YouTube channel, embed new videos on the server or link to them along with your thoughts about the topic. If you use Instagram, import a selection of images to interest your readers further.

Cross-pollination is a powerful tool and works in both directions. If you have speaking events, readings, or other events away from Discord, make sure you post reminders about this both in your subscription service and on Discord, and consider inviting these outside audiences to your server. In your author business, there's always room to grow. ■

Wendy Van Camp

Wendy Van Camp

Wendy Van Camp is the Poet Laureate for the City of Anaheim, California. Her work is influenced by cutting edge technology, astronomy, and daydreams. A graduate of the Ad Astra Speculative Fiction Workshop, Wendy is a nominated finalist for the Elgin Award, for the Pushcart Prize, and for a Dwarf Stars Award. Her poems, stories, and articles have appeared in: "Starlight Scifaiku Review", "The Junction", "Quantum Visions", and other literary journals. She is the poet and illustrator of "The Planets: a scifaiku poetry collection" and editor of the annual anthology "Eccentric Orbits: An Anthology of Science Fiction Poetry". Find her at https://wendyvancamp.com

Shifting Magic

THE MANY PUBLISHING LIVES OF SKYE MACKINNON

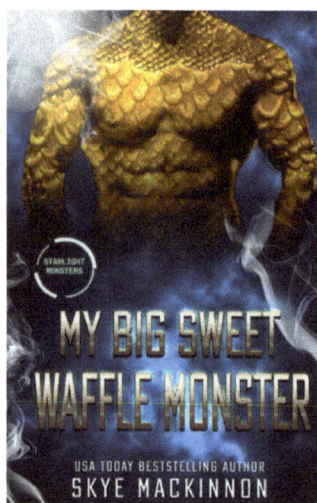

Never mind that Skye MacKinnon shares her Scotch heritage, teaching ability, and calm courage in the face of a changing world with J.K. Rowling's Professor McGonagall. Or that MacKinnon's cat never appeared during our interview, so spectacle-shaped markings around the cat's eyes—like those on McGonagall's feline form—cannot be ruled out. According to MacKinnon, before she began her own publishing journey, authors, in her eyes, were akin to "mystical beings."

Of course, these days, MacKinnon—McGonagall comparisons aside—seems like a mystical being in her own right, to her readers and to other authors. She's well known in the Wide For The Win community (https://www.wideforthewin.com), where she serves on the board as community director. She also founded a Facebook Group to provide resources for indie authors marketing German language translations of their books (https://facebook.com/groups/marketinggermanbooks). In her own author career, MacKinnon has published sixty-six adult novels and co-written thirty adult novels, four short stories/novellas, and eleven anthologies. She's also published sixteen picture books, including one nonfiction title, and a young adult novel, all in a range of genres and under a variety of pen names.

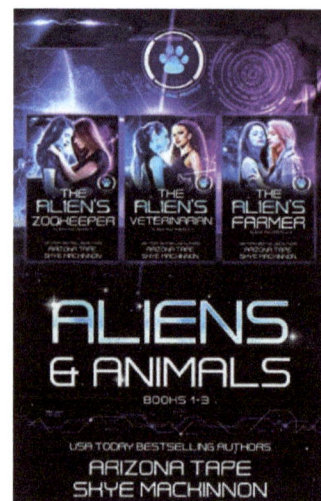

A SERIES OF PUBLISHING 'ACCIDENTS'

MacKinnon's publishing journey began "in a series of accidents," she says. While she'd always loved writing, others had convinced her that "author" wasn't a proper job. So she chose a career in journalism, working first as a science specialist and later in communications. Then, in 2013, after losing a bet, she "had to write a story—quite a spicy story—about cavemen … [that] taught me my first bits and pieces about self-publishing." At that time, self-publishing was still limited to the Smashwords distributor, and authors had to format their works using the platform's original and infamous file formatting tool, colloquially dubbed the "meatgrinder." Not unlike a dragon, the "meatgrinder" accepted files formatted to its excruciatingly exact standards and spawned e-books for all imaginable devices. MacKinnon's ability to tame this legendary beast could be argued to be nothing short of magical.

Four years later, in 2017, her first book took off. "Suddenly, I had fans and readers and a Facebook Group and a newsletter. Basically, I had to learn very quickly, because everything was happening so fast." Nota bene: That book was called *Meow*, and it's still her bestselling book and series across languages.

Without worrying about paperbacks, other retailers, or other formats like audiobook, she published on Amazon with Kindle Select and focused on writing the next books. "In retrospect," the former journalist says, "I wish I'd done a lot more research."

But she also agreed that skipping it might have actually helped her early publishing efforts. "If people do the bare minimum and somehow succeed with that, then it can still work," she says. "It does help if you have savings or support from other people. It probably doesn't work in [the] Reverse Harem [genre] anymore. I was in the gold rush."

MacKinnon's first book replaced her day job's income after a few months, and she went to part time at six months. She still had no plans to become a full-time author. Then, at nine months, her work contract expired. Instead of looking for a new job, she gave herself a trial year to write full time.

"Luckily, it worked out," she says, "and I've never looked back. I always tell people, 'Don't be hasty. Do it one step at a time, and think about all the consequences if it doesn't work out.' I was lucky."

In addition to luck, she had insider knowledge of her writing genres. "I always write what I read," she says. "That's why the genres I write change … from Time Travel to Aliens to Historical to Contemporary and Fantasy and you name it." Despite hitting the gold rush with the Reverse Harem genre, she leaves room for the muse. "I don't want to be as rational about [the choice of genre] because I want the characters and the worlds to be the important thing."

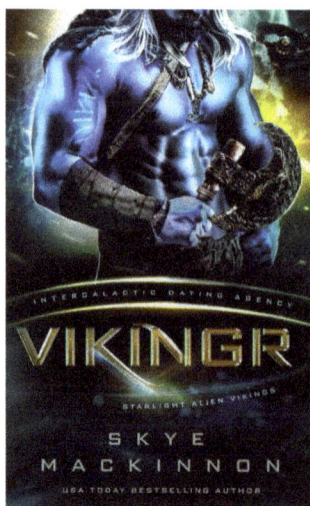

PUBLISHING A UNICORN

In Christmas 2018, MacKinnon's email newsletter for readers of her adult novels included "this tiny wee story about how a unicorn side character came to be," she explains. "He's not a shifter, he's an actual unicorn, and he's quite sassy and snarky, and people just have always liked him and wanted more." Replies from newsletter subscribers, however, were confusing. Instead of professing their own adoration for the story, many responded, "My kids love this!"

True to form, she experimented to find out if this unicorn was a fluke. "I made some illustrations … published it under a new name, and suddenly, I was a children's book author." It was no fluke. By November 2023, MacKinnon had finished her seventeenth or possibly eighteenth picture book, which she publishes under the pen name Isla Wynter. Fun fact: the pen name draws two character names from her other book series.

With no children of her own, MacKinnon claims she wasn't "well placed" to write children's books, but she happens to have an excellent source of insider information. Her sister, a primary school teacher, regularly fills her in on the kids' favorite animals. MacKinnon quips, "Sloths are apparently on trend."

A WHISKERHOOD OF AUTHORS

Early in 2017, MacKinnon joined forces with a small group—first six authors, then four—and collaborated on writing projects, anthologies, and book signings. Besides finding and filtering new opportunities, the group became friends who have chatted every day for the last six years. "We all saved a lot of time and effort," she says.

While acknowledging the value of groups that include authors with advanced skills, MacKinnon says, "In the beginning, I think it's way more important to have people who are at the same stage or only slightly more advanced. You can grow easier that way."

MAGICAL POWERS IN INTERNATIONAL MARKETS

In 2020, once her bestselling series came out as audiobooks, MacKinnon applied her formidable research and communication powers—in two languages—to German translations and the question of how best to publish them. "It's definitely a journalism thing. If I don't know something, I will find out," she says.

Her habit of emailing sources directly works well for early access to information. "You never know in advance if this will be actually worth it or if it will be a ten-hour waste of time," she says of the research required to check out a new opportunity. But she admits, "I do find little nuggets of gold."

By the time her first German translation was released, she was getting steady requests to turn her knowledge into a book. Wryly, she notes that *Self-Publishing in German: How to Translate, Publish, and Market Your Books,* which came out in 2021, took much longer than expected. One frustration unique to nonfiction was how quickly, and confidentially, new features appeared. A major new feature—print books—for Tolino, the largest German distributor of e-books, was announced the day after her book came out. "But to be fair, they had shared several other things," she says.

A second edition of the book will have to wait, because recent health issues have limited MacKinnon's work time to an average of an hour a day. But even this unplanned reduction in hours was a useful "experiment" for this self-identified workaholic.

Before her illness, she says she was "scared to go on holiday for a week." Now, she has proof that "if you get your system right and … routine in place, it's possible to take off a long time and not see a massive drop in income."

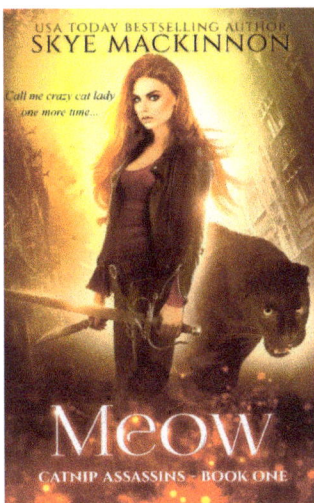

WEIRD AND WONDERFUL GENRE SHIFTER

Currently, MacKinnon has four to five "main" pen names, evidence of her creativity, productivity, and her ability to shift gears. Skye B. MacKinnon is her nonfiction pen name, and Skye MacKinnon is for Adult Romance, her "main breadwinner" accounting for 80 percent of her time. She writes in so many subgenres that she's developed a handy quiz for readers looking for their next book: https://skyemackinnon.com/index.html.

Her children's book pen name, Isla Wynter, takes the lead from Halloween to Christmas. She reports that her best-selling Isla Wynter book is *The Little Ghost Who Didn't Like to Be Scary* but that *The Pink Ghost* may soon overtake it. She adds, "I've never had this many Halloween sales. It's ridiculous."

Her secret pen name is used for "other weird Erotica since [the cavemen], but mostly because I lose bets or it's a challenge or is for charity … [like] the Australian wildfires." An older shared pen name has been retired, and a new pen name is in the works for her first crime novel.

"I love an experiment," she says, "which is why I think my writing style and the things I write about change quite often." Her "best ever best-selling book" was an experiment—a cute premade

SKYE MACKINNON

MOTHER OF GODS

A WINTER PRINCESS PREQUEL

cover inspired a book that was "so out there and so weird." She didn't expect it to find readers, but it was published in three languages and featured in bookstores. "Sometimes," she says, "you will be pleasantly surprised. Sometimes you will be terribly disappointed. … It's definitely worth trying because you will never find out what could have been."

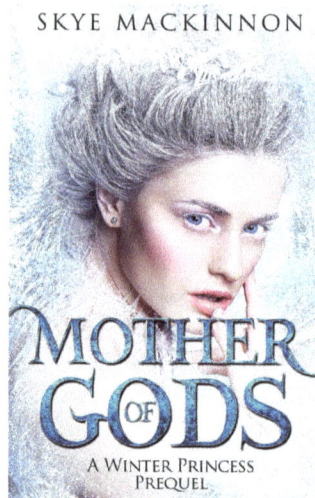

Alongside her own writing, MacKinnon offers author consultations at https://perytonpress.com/consultations. As a mentor, she is willing to experiment to discover the truth about new publishing opportunities and shares her discoveries generously. Her extensive backlist also gives her the freedom to organize charity anthologies or do other time-intensive activities that don't pay for themselves. "Herding authors," she says. "It's worse than herding cats." With a smile hinting at deep and mystical knowledge, MacKinnon adds, "I have a cat."

It's enough to remind one of a certain beloved Hogwarts professor, and though MacKinnon may not teach wizardry or witchcraft, her career thus far has been nothing short of magical.

Like Harry Potter's Professor McGonagall, MacKinnon has secret identities, magical publishing powers, and a feline inquisitiveness. Is it mere coincidence that her cat, Valkyrie, didn't appear during our conversation? ■

Laurel Decher

Laurel Decher

There might be no frigate like a book, but publishing can feel like a voyage on the H.M.S. Surprise. There's always a twist and there's never a moment to lose. Laurel's mission is to help you make the most of today's opportunities. She's a strategic problem-solver, tool collector, and co-inventor of the "you never know" theory of publishing. As an epidemiologist, she studied factors that help babies and toddlers thrive. Now she writes books for children ages nine to twelve about finding more magic in life. She's a member of the Society for Children's Book Writers and Illustrators (SCBWI), has various advanced degrees, and a tendency to smuggle vegetables into storylines.

PLANNING TRAVEL TO A CONFERENCE?

Use miles.

Explore ways to make the most of your award miles.

Writelink.to/unitedair

Buzz from the Beach
A LOOK BACK AT THE NINC 2023 CONFERENCE

At the TradeWinds Island Grand Beach Resort in St. Pete Beach, Florida, September 20–24, 2023, the professional novelists organization dubbed Novelists Inc. (NINC) put on their annual conference laden with conversations about the modern publishing landscape. NINC is a professional writer's networking organization designed to help manage an author's career—an industry familiar with rapid-onset change. At conferences like NINC, upcoming shifts in technology, tactics, and strategies often come up. NINC 2023 was no different; in fact, it seemed to embrace these shifts in the industry, not just in individual sessions but also in the conference's overall theme.

Tawdra Kandle, who is the assistant conference director and programming chair for the annual conference, shared her thoughts on the event from both a programming perspective and as someone who sat in on a few of the sessions. "The theme of NINC 2023 was Elevate!," Kandle says. "The main focus under that heading was discovering the paths forward for taking our publishing careers to the next level." Naturally, this included discussions on some of the more buzzworthy topics in the industry today, including artificial intelligence (AI) and the direct sales model.

Kandle says sessions at NINC events are geared toward qualifying authors as much as established authors and are not discriminatory as to the avenue an author chooses to publish. Although the organization works hard to present content that's applicable to everyone, she notes that at least three-quarters or more of the workshops would appeal directly to independently published authors. Alongside more timely discussions about AI and direct sales models that took place this year, Kandle says less technical topics such as author burnout and exhaustion were also explored. Authors can sometimes tend to overlook such topics; having intentional sessions to call out these issues increases the likelihood that someone might identify these struggles within themselves.

When asked about specific sessions Kandle attended, she identified a few sessions that were standouts for her.

"As a member of the conference team, I'm often not able to attend all of the sessions I'd like, but I was very impressed by Sarra Cannon's presentation on the path back to joy, Erica Ridley's masterclass on newsletters, and Melanie Harlow's workshop on staying in your lane without getting stuck in a rut," she says. "Overall, I feel the conference offered valuable content to help authors grow in a well-rounded, positive manner—not just sales or marketing, not just producing books rapidly, but how to maintain our vibrant careers for the long term."

The NINC conference had a clear intention to include both craft sessions and business sessions for authors and publishers in attendance, and Kandle says that was by design. The necessity to produce well-written books never goes away, she says, going so far as to call producing subpar books "a disservice not only to our reading audience but also to our author community." It all seemed to match well with the conference's overall theme—Elevate!—the idea being to lift authors up and discover paths forward for taking publishing careers to the next level.

Much like other popular author conferences, NINC attempts to create a blueprint by which all authors can mold their business model. This strategy revolves around good books, good business, and good intent to lift your author colleagues. There is something to be said for consistency of messaging, and NINC as an organization seems to have just that.

The NINC 2023 conference topics certainly reflected it, according to Kandle, and if past years are to be a guide, authors can expect more of the same in the 2024 rendition of the event. Next year's conference takes place September 18–22, also in St. Pete Beach; watch the organization's website, https://ninc.com, for updates and more information on how to register. ◼

David Viergutz

David Viergutz

David Viergutz is a disabled Army Veteran, Law Enforcement Veteran, husband and proud father. He is an author of stories from every flavor of horror and dark fiction. One day, David's wife sat him down and gave him the confidence to start putting his imagination on paper. From then on out his creativity has no longer been stifled by self-doubt and he continues to write with a smile on his face in a dark, candle-lit room.

Writing 'The End' on the Story of 20Books Vegas

TWO CONFERENCES COLLIDE AS 20BOOKS VEGAS TRANSITIONS TO AUTHOR NATION

During the second week of November, the largest group of independent authors, publishers, and industry professionals gathered at the Horseshoe casino hotel in Las Vegas, Nevada. It was the sixth iteration of the event in seven years, yet it had a much different air than in years past. Following a post on Facebook in July 2023 that had announced the news, event-goers were attending this year's conference knowing it would be the final show under the 20BooksTo50K® moniker. Craig Martelle, indie powerhouse and co-founder of 20BooksTo50K®, was stepping aside, not stepping down, as the conference director, and with it, the convention—20Books Vegas—was shifting hands to a new consortium of authors and industry leaders.

Throughout the week, the main question that seemed to permeate the atmosphere was what this new conference was going to be like. Would there be tears and hugs farewell? Or would it feel like another page turned in the story of the indie author community? There was a bit of it all, actually. Those questions and fears were addressed in a tear-jerker moment between 20BooksTo50K® co-founder Michael Anderle and Martelle during their closing keynote speech, which was followed by a standing ovation. Martelle clarified that 20BooksTo50K® would live on in spirit and in the Facebook Group, though the conference was changing.

20Books Vegas was becoming Author Nation, led by a team of industry professionals and headed by Joe Solari, who could dedicate the time and resources necessary to take the conference to the next level. Martelle explained in further detail what this would look like, including a reveal of the all-star cast that would serve to run Author Nation. This introduction included Chelle Honiker, publisher of *Indie Author Magazine*, who will serve as the content committee chair. Martelle advised the values of 20BooksTo50K® would be infused in the guiding principles of Author Nation, given who was selected to lead the conference.

The shift reflected what the rest of the conference had been for many. There weren't any goodbyes, only plans for the next year. There wasn't a sigh of disappointment at the closure of the 20Books chapter of the Vegas event but a collective energy of "What comes next?" Martelle said publicly at the event he wouldn't be disappearing completely. He'd still be a part of 20BooksTo50K®. He'd still be speaking at Author Nation's event, and he'd still be writing books. When he did a live reading of his book during the Readers & Authors Vegas Event (RAVE) Friday, November 10, he did so proudly. As he stood over a cake on Saturday, November 11, to celebrate the Marine Corps' birthday, he smiled. The changing of the guard from 20Books Vegas to Author Nation wasn't bittersweet. There was nothing bitter about it.

It was just different. And like many an article about adapting to the changes we face in publishing, so was the air about the conference. Change was coming. It was coming in artificial intelligence, in direct sales, in translations, and in the conference. But few vocalized the feeling of being disrupted by the change of name, leadership, or direction of the conference. Most, it seemed, were just happy to know 20Books Vegas would continue, if only in spirit.

Honiker shared her thoughts about Author Nation 2024 and beyond and outlined a few changes that would be implemented right away. From a bird's-eye view, she noted a focus on the division of beginning, intermediate, and advanced topics and speakers. She noted a larger focus on the RAVE event, making it both attractive for authors and readers alike, and the introduction of special guests, such as director, screenwriter, and comic book writer Kevin Smith, who will deliver a keynote address ahead of RAVE 2024.

It all represents what 20Books Vegas was about, and what Author Nation will be about: independent writers and entrepreneurs looking to make a living from their work. As the 20Books Vegas event comes to an end and Author Nation's Vegas conference takes its place, the spirit of 20BooksTo50K® and the indie author community it has fostered remains alive and well, and attendees seem excited for a new chapter. ■

David Viergutz

David Viergutz

David Viergutz is a disabled Army Veteran, Law Enforcement Veteran, husband and proud father. He is an author of stories from every flavor of horror and dark fiction. One day, David's wife sat him down and gave him the confidence to start putting his imagination on paper. From then on out his creativity has no longer been stifled by self-doubt and he continues to write with a smile on his face in a dark, candle-lit room.

The Author Impact

WRITERS REFLECT ON MARTELLE'S CONFERENCE LEGACY

Interviewing attendees at the 2023 20Books Vegas conference, the final iteration of the event by 20BooksTo50K® co-founder and conference organizer Craig Martelle after seven years, it is clear this conference has not only transformed lives; it has transformed the indie author industry. By creating a safe space for introverted authors to connect with a like-minded and determined cohort of professionals, this event has expanded authors' voices in the publishing marketplace.

Information and connection have built confidence in the industry. "The first conference at Sam's Town showed me how many people were doing what I was doing," says Historical Fiction author J. Clifton Slater, nearly dancing. "I had two books out. Other people had one or two books out. Some people had twenty books out. We were like: 'Eh, we're not like them,' but you know what? I am like them. I now have thirty-seven novels out." Slater, like many authors who have attended 20BooksTo50K® events in Vegas over the years, is a happy human.

Two thousand happy introverts at various levels of their author journey make for a unique environment—a reunion of like minds and souls, all focused on subverting the dominant publishing paradigm. As the community says goodbye to the 20Books Vegas conference and prepares for a new version of the event under Author Nation's leadership, several authors share their reflections on what the past six events under the 20BooksTo50K® banner has meant to them and to their careers.

BUILDING COMMUNITY

Gerald M. Kilby learned about 20Books five years ago and has attended 20Books London, Madrid, Amsterdam, Edinburgh, and, as of this year, Vegas. "Writing is a lonely business. What makes this event so good is the sharing of information, regardless of if you're a top bestseller or if you're a newbie author, or if you haven't written a book at all," he says. "Everybody's in this together." Kilby has been writing Science Fiction novels for over seven years and had stumbled into success before discovering 20Books. "I didn't understand how or why I was successful. When I came to my first 20Books event, I began to understand what I was doing right, where I could improve, and [to gain] the confidence to go full time."

Mystery writer Deann Powell had several books published before attending 20Books Vegas and has attended all but the first event in Las Vegas. "Going to the conference for five years has boosted my personal life," Powell says. "It has been a fantastic place to meet people who have become some of my best friends. We all write in different genres, and sometimes that's really helpful too—getting someone's perspective from a completely different genre."

Just being able to connect in person with other authors from all around the world makes a difference for some. "It changed my life. It showed me that I wasn't alone," Slater says, "and it gave me the confidence to do something I've always wanted to do."

Kilby agrees. "If you're a writer or just starting out as a writer, it's a very lonely business. Often, nobody at home gets you. … Nobody understands you. So when you come to something like 20Books, you realize that all these people understand what you're talking about."

It is this common language and love for writing and publishing, and this sense of connection, that brings people back over and over and helps support others on their journey.

THE GIVING CONFERENCE

Conference attendees' gifts to one another might be the most profound but often silent ways of giving back. Tables are covered with pins and stickers and bling with which to decorate their lanyards. Attendees might bring Hawaiian leis to share, or buy drinks for those new to the conference. These small acts together create the love-fest of 20Books Vegas, with each of us lifting one another up as we climb our individual mountains.

Vendors and successful authors alike have donated funds to give back as well. Martelle made sure that no one went without. Subway and CVS gift cards, as well as cash envelopes, were available for those who were in a financial pinch. As of Martelle's latest Facebook post about scholarships, fifty-seven scholarships to attend this year's conference were given away—to the tune of $37,277.82.

These scholarships to attend the conference have shifted mindsets and lifted spirits. For Siobhan Purcell, a Cozy Mystery writer, winning a scholarship three years ago allowed her to meet her tribe. "This is my third year in a row now [attending the conference]. I wish I could say that it's made me finish my book, but it has given me more focus. I've connected with some absolutely incredible people and I know … if I put the work in what is achievable. That's been life changing in itself." Her confidence in the business, and in herself, has grown each year she has attended, she says. When she returns to Vegas next year for Author Nation's first event, it will be with her own book in hand.

Some attendees had already written their books but still desired industry knowledge, and a scholarship changed everything for them. Claire K. Clement—this author's younger sister and an academic historian—was not sure the indie path was for her, though she has followed the 20Books

Facebook page for a few years now. When she was offered a scholarship—and a shared room with her sister—she couldn't say no. "I'm very grateful to have received the scholarship. It's changed my perspective and opened my mind to the possibilities of making a living at this and a real sense of how to approach my business and genre writing well enough to make it a career," she says.

MINDSET SHIFTS

The most common attendee takeaway is that of a massive mindset shift. "Something I always heard was: don't be a waiting writer, be a working writer," says Bokerah Brumley, an Urban Fantasy and Paranormal Romance writer who has attended three Vegas events and describes the event as an amazing place to learn what is possible. "I've been publishing since 2015, but Kate Pickford gave me some pointers on hooks and how to connect with readers in a different way that really rocketed my writing to a different level."

Whether people heard something in a session, in a hallway conversation, or over drinks with new friends, the conference has given many a place to expand creatively. This expansion carries over into their personal lives.

Paul Ian Cross, who has attended events since 2019, is a prolific academic and children's science writer. However, following the 2022 Vegas conference, he felt a mindset shift. "It's made me realize what I can achieve, and learning about mindset here has been key for me. In the past, I haven't manifested what I wanted, and the more positive my mindset has grown, I am now getting where I needed to go." This year, Cross walked in with one plan and left with a bigger, brighter, better idea for his author business. This is the mindset shift many authors seemed to encounter—an ever-increasing understanding and expansion of themselves and their careers.

MOVING FORWARD

Slater describes the growth of the 20Books Vegas conference in terms of swag. "I found out about the 20Books conference the first year, and I called Craig. He needed somewhere to drop-ship to. The first year, everything that was delivered could fit in my car. This year, the pile of swag was bigger than my car." Slater explained that enough swag filled his garage that they needed six cars to transport the goods to the 2023 event.

The mountain of event swag is but a fraction of the physical evidence that Martelle and his team have pulled together over the years. From notebooks filled with quotes, ideas, and contact information from various events to the vendors' promotional pens, books written by friends, lanyards carried home, and headshots by Arpit Mehta, many authors' lives have become filled with reminders of 20BooksTo50K®.

These reminders will remain with us as the conference is handed over to Author Nation, led by Joe Solari and his consortium. Author Nation promises to expand upon what the 20BooksVegas conference brought to the world of indie publishing. Hallway conversations at 20Books Vegas were peppered with possibilities of this new conference mixed with gratitude for Martelle and all that he and his team have done for the indie author tribe.

Martelle has often spoken of wanting to do the work of 20BooksTo50K® and the conference to balance his life's experiences. Now that he closes out his tenure as director of the largest indie author conference in the world, does he feel he has completed his mission to give back to humanity? In a rare quiet moment of repose, he sat back in a chair with his feet up on the second day of the conference. "I gave everything that I have to the group members, and people ask: how can we thank you for helping us?" He replies, "You can thank me by being successful. There's seventy-five plus thousand members, with over thirty thousand who are active. I've done what I needed to do, and we have a whole generation of authors—no matter the age—who can carry on."

In the final moments of 20Books Vegas 2023, Martelle handed off the conference to Solari and Author Nation. In his final conference gift to all of us, he opened the doorway to the future of indies to let our tribe pass through. ■

Heather Clement Davis

Heather Clement Davis

Heather Clement Davis has twenty-six years' experience in museums, archaeology, art, counseling, art therapy, creative writing, and nonprofit management. She holds enough graduate work to make a Ph.D. cry as her neurodivergent brain is hooked on learning everything. She's currently a masters candidate in Arts Management. Her paintings and pottery are in galleries and collections worldwide and her poetry and her nonfiction and fiction has found its way to literary journals around the U.S. When not writing or making art, Heather can be found playing Catan or watching Star Trek with her family.

What We Know about What's Next

THE TRANSITION FROM 20BOOKS VEGAS TO AUTHOR NATION

20Books Vegas, held November 6-10 at the Horseshoe Las Vegas casino hotel, was the largest conference for indie authors in 2023, attracting more than two thousand five hundred attendees. Ten tracks of sessions covered topics such as marketing, audio, craft, and business, led by industry experts like Joanna Penn, John Truby, Ines Johnson, Bryan Cohen, and dozens more. Since 2017, 20Books Vegas has been an excellent in-person networking opportunity for indie authors and offered insights to the industry for those attending virtually. Following the event, most of this year's sessions have been made available on YouTube for those who could not attend in person at https://youtube.com/@20Booksto50kRLiveEvents.

2023 was the last year for 20Books Vegas, however, as co-founder Craig Martelle, who has led and coordinated the show since its inception, announced in July he is stepping away to focus on health issues. For 2024, the conference, now called Author Nation, will be led by Joe Solari—who taught several sessions at 20Books on successfully running an author business—as well as a consortium made up of leaders in the indie publishing community. Chelle Honiker, publisher of *Indie Author Magazine*, is also among the consortium as the content committee chair.

Many 20Books Vegas attendees have questions about Author Nation, and Solari's company, Author Ventures LLC, has created a website, https://www.AuthorNation.live, for interested parties to sign up to receive updates.

WHAT ISN'T CHANGING FOR AUTHOR NATION 2024

Author Nation will take place at the same venue as 20Books Vegas, Horseshoe Las Vegas. It will be the same time of the year as 20Books: November 11-15, 2024. The cost for authors to attend in person will still be $399.99.

Like 20Books Vegass 2023, an Author Nation ticket will cover attendance for Monday's Industry Expo, author education sessions Tuesday through Thursday, and admission to the Reader & Author Vegas Event (RAVE) on Friday.

THE PHILOSOPHY OF AUTHOR NATION

Even with several similarities, "Author Nation is not the same conference with a new name," Solari says. "Michael Anderle owns the trademark for the name '20Books,' and his team is planning other events with the 20Books name. Author Ventures LLC assumed the liability of the event contract from Craig Martelle, and we all support each other going forward, but we're no longer part of 20Books."

Authors will see a philosophical change in the Author Nation conferences. "Let's figure out what your best life through writing is," Solari says. "It's great if you want to be a seven-figure author, but that might not be the best way for your writing career to serve you. How do you build your best writing career? Kindle Unlimited, going wide, Kickstarter, subscriptions—there are a multitude of pros and cons, and it's our job to help you navigate success with an approach that best suits your goals, personality, and business."

In Author Nation emails and social media communications, Solari outlines his vision that value in publishing is created in the connection between authors and readers.

A major change will be how Author Nation markets RAVE to readers and book buyers. The Author Nation team is prioritizing growing attendance to the event on Friday, November 15. "I want authors to sell ten times what they sold in 2023," Solari says. To attract readers, Author Nation will host a keynote for Author Nation and RAVE attendees the night before RAVE, November 14, 2024, with indie filmmaker Kevin Smith (*Clerks, Dogma, Jay and Silent Bob Strike Back*).

LIVE-STREAMING AND DIGITAL TICKETS

In a November 15, 2023, communication, Solari stated that Author Nation will not offer a lives-tream option in 2024. "If you only included the livestream attendees, 20Books would still have been the biggest author conference of the year," Solari says. "In past years, the same people who were trying to make sure the event was going smoothly for the live attendees were also slammed with issues from the livestreaming." At the 2023 show, technical issues made several of the sessions unwatchable remotely.

"A livestream event is something we want to offer in the future," Solari says, but "the team doesn't have the bandwidth to support it in 2024."

Instead, Author Nation will offer a digital ticket to access recorded videos after the conference. While 20Books offered videos on YouTube after the show for no cost, Author Nation will require a digital ticket to view sessions and other content. "We can focus on the recording quality and post-production to make the videos the highest quality possible," says Solari. Ticket holders will have access to an extended Q&A after each session. Solari calls these remote sessions "after-parties." Speakers and vendors have been positive about the idea, Solari said, because it will give them the ability to give complete, thoughtful answers without being pressed for time.

HELPING AUTHORS GROW THEIR CAREERS

"One of the goals of Author Nation 2024 is to ensure that Author Nation attendees will be in a better place in their career the next year," Solari says. "We want the 2024 attendee who has never published to have written and published their book in 2025. We want the author who is losing money in 2024 to break even or be profitable in 2025.

"We have great DNA from 20Books Vegas, and Author Nation includes a team of people that are being thoughtful about what the author community needs for the next three to five years," he says.

Although attendees should expect significant differences from 20Books Vegas, the conference will continue to prioritize author success. "We're doing this because we believe there's more than one right answer," Solari says. "Author Nation is the place to come to collect the information and make that decision for yourself and your author business." ◼

Paul Austin Ardoin

Paul Austin Ardoin

Paul Austin Ardoin is the USA TODAY bestselling indie author of The Fenway Stevenson Mysteries and The Woodhead & Becker Mysteries. He holds a B.A. in creative writing from the University of California, Santa Barbara and an M.B.A. in marketing from the University of Phoenix. His book Zero to Four Figures: Making $1,000 a Month with Self-Published Fiction is scheduled for publication in June 2023.

What's in Store for 2024?

PREVIEW THIS YEAR'S CALENDAR OF EVENTS FOR INDIE AUTHORS

One of the highs of being an indie author is connecting with like-minded people, and the best places to do that are conferences and retreats. From broad-scope conferences covering everything from craft to marketing to smaller retreats, the industry has a range of events that will appeal to every author. And no matter which you choose to attend, you are practically guaranteed to come away with ideas and inspiration for your writing career, along with new friendships to sustain you along the way.

This year, author-focused events will span the globe from Scranton, Pennsylvania, to Seville, Spain—and if your travel budget is tight, there are plenty of virtual options scheduled for you to enjoy from the comfort of your writing desk as well. So what better way to break in our calendars for the new year than rounding up some of the biggest indie author conferences scheduled in 2024? The list below offers a broad overview of events that will appeal to any indie author, but be sure to search for additional, more genre-specific events at https://indieauthortools.com/conferences.

INDIE PUB NOLA:

When: January 28–31, 2024
Where: New Orleans, Louisiana
Cost: $850
Space for this year's event is full, but keep an eye on the Indie Pub Facebook Group for updates or information about future events.

AUTHOR SUSTAINABILITY CONFERENCE:

When: February 2–4, 2024
Where: Dublin, Ireland
Cost: €260
For an invitation to register, fill out the form at https://authorsustainability.com/asc2024.

SUPERSTARS WRITING SEMINARS:

When: February 7–10, 2024
Where: Colorado Springs, Colorado
Cost: $899.99

Registration is open now. Visit https://superstarswriting.com for more information and to view the schedule of events.

PLOTTING IN PARADISE WRITING RETREAT:

When: February 4–14, 2024
Where: Bali, Indonesia
Cost: $3,500
Visit https://plottinginparadise.com for more information.

AUTHOR ALCHEMY SUMMIT:

When: February 22–25, 2024
Where: Portland, Oregon
Cost: $899

Registration is open now. Visit https://authoralchemysummit.com to learn more or to sign up.

THE FUTURE OF PUBLISHING MASTERMIND:

When: February 26–29, 2024
Where: New Orleans, Louisiana
Cost: $2,999 for in-person event, $499 for virtual option
Learn more and register at https://thefutureofpublishingmastermind.com.

20BOOKS SEVILLE:

When: March 8 and 9, 2024
Where: Seville, Spain
Cost: €279

Registration is open now. Find out more at http://20booksspain.com/en.

INDIE INSPIRATION:

When: March 28–30, 2024 (online content will be accessible until May 4, 2024)
Where: Virtual
Cost: $399
Find out more information and register at https://indie-inspiration.teachable.com/p/indiecon2024.

INDIE PUB SCRANTON (BEGINNER'S WORKSHOP):

When: April 27, 2024
Where: Scranton, Pennsylvania
Cost: $150
Space for this event is limited. To submit your application, fill out the interest form at https://forms.gle/M1JkNGjiRJVCwX677.

TORONTO INDIE AUTHOR'S CONFERENCE:

When: May 4 and 5, 2024
Where: Toronto, Ontario, Canada
Cost: $120 CAD + taxes
Find out more and register at https://torontoindieauthorcon.com.

SUBSCRIPTIONS FOR AUTHORS SUMMIT:

When: May 6 and 7, 2024
Where: Boston, Massachusetts
Cost: $199 as early access pricing to the in-person event, and $49 for a virtual ticket
Learn more and register at https://summit.subscriptionsforauthors.com. Space is limited, so sign up early if you're interested.

INKERS CON:

When: June 7–9, 2024, with access to the digital conference July 20–August 2, 2024
Where: Dallas, Texas
Cost: $649, or $249 for the digital event. Early bird sign-ups for the digital event are discounted to $199 for a limited time.
Learn more and register at https://www.inkerscon.com.

SELF PUBLISHING SHOW LIVE:

When: June 25 and 26, 2024, with a virtual version of the event July 23 and 24, 2024
Where: London, UK
Cost: £175–£210 for the in-person event
Registration is open now for both the digital and in-person events. Find out more at https://selfpublishingformula.com/spslive.

WHEN WORDS COLLIDE:

When: August 16–18, 2024
Where: Calgary, Alberta, Canada
Cost: $60 CAD, with prices increasing February 1, 2024
Ticket availability for the festival is limited. Visit https://alexandrawriters.org/when-words-collide-2024.html to learn more or to sign up.

NOVELISTS, INC. (NINC) CONFERENCE:

When: September 18–22, 2024
Where: St. Pete Beach, Florida
Cost: Open to Novelists, Inc. members only
Find out more at https://ninc.com/conferences/future-conferences.

AUTHOR NATION CONFERENCE:

When: November 11–15, 2024
Where: Las Vegas, Nevada
Cost: $399.99
Registration will open in January. Sign up to be on the mailing list at https://www.authornation.live to receive updates and information as it's announced.

Which events are you planning on attending in 2024? Do you know of any others we should include? Reach out to us at Events@indieauthormagazine.com! ■

Robyn Sarty

Robyn Sarty

Robyn Sarty is the author of two novels and several short stories, and manages her own publishing company. She loves helping other authors with their books and can often be found nerding out over story elements with her friends. She spent five years as a project coordinator for an international engineering firm, and now uses those skills to chase writers instead of engineers and hopes it will be good training for her first marathon. Growing up as a third culture kid, books were the one constant in her life, and as such, Robyn believes that books are portals to the magic that lies within, and authors are wielders of that magic. She also admits to being a staunch, loyal, and unabashed supporter of the Oxford comma.

'Go Your Own Way'

FOUR DIRECT SALES PLATFORMS TO MATCH YOUR BUSINESS NEEDS

The "Rumours" are true. Indie authors can earn more revenue and drive better engagement through direct sales. And as indie authors increasingly look to expand their reach through wide publication, it makes sense to consider following Fleetwood Mac's call to "go your own way."

You might not be ready to break up with Amazon yet, but if you're looking for a more open relationship, maybe it's time to set aside that bully romance for more of a "why choose" option. Going direct—selling books through their own distribution channels, such as through their author website or in person—brings some authors the control they crave.

The best part is that it doesn't have to be an all-or-nothing shift in your business plan. Keep reading to explore a few of the ways you can add direct sales to your existing author business.

Etsy

YOU WANT TO HAVE A STORE, BUT YOU DON'T WANT TO BUILD IT: ETSY

For authors looking to dip a toe into direct sales without learning a new platform, Etsy offers an easy first step. It's similar to Amazon in that it doesn't require much setup beyond loading in your products, and to a certain extent, it's a marketplace with a built-in customer base. People are already going there to shop, so author marketing is less about convincing readers to buy and more about convincing them to choose your book over other products the Etsy algorithm shows them.

The standard plan has no monthly charges, and you can upgrade to Etsy Plus and get more features for $10 per month. However, Etsy has so many sales fees that people have developed third-party calculators to help sellers track them. For example: every new listing, or re-listing of a sold product, costs twenty cents, every order carries a 6.5 percent transaction fee, and payment processing fees are 3 percent plus twenty-five cents per transaction.

Keep in mind that you will also need to account for order fulfillment, whether you choose to purchase your books in bulk and mail them out yourself or integrate a print-on-demand service like Lulu Direct, BookVault, or TheBookPatch.com.

An author with a smaller catalog, who is willing to part with some of their profit in order to have someone else handle taxes, calculate shipping, and provide secure transactions, might do well starting with Etsy. Authors can even link their Etsy shop with Squarespace or Shopify as their business grows.

Forbes recently compared Shopify and Etsy in more detail.

YOU WANT TO DESIGN AND RUN YOUR OWN STORE: SHOPIFY

Shopify is widely considered the easiest e-commerce platform. Its customization features provide so many options that some users, like best-selling Romance author Jillian Dodd, have completely replaced their traditional websites with a Shopify store. Shopify also integrates with WordPress, Squarespace, and Wix, so you don't have to let go of your home base to get started.

Unlike Etsy, Shopify charges a monthly subscription fee, in addition to transaction fees when you make a sale. They offer three tiers at $29, $79, and $299 per month. The lowest tier is the most popular, and probably more than enough for most authors starting out in direct sales. According to Shopify's sales page, at this level, you get "everything you need to create your store, ship products, and process payments." The higher tiers allow for more staff accounts and more customized reports.

Users cite customer support, ease of customization, and data collection as reasons to switch to Spotify. Although Etsy allows customers to "favorite" your shop and products, the marketplace doesn't collect customer emails. On Shopify, customers can opt in at checkout, allowing you to follow up with marketing newsletters and store updates. Buyers can save their information so they don't need to re-enter it when making purchases from another Shopify store, making Shop Pay payments as trusted as Google Pay or Apple Pay.

You can also get the best of both worlds by integrating your Etsy shop with Shopify. The Shopify app will synchronize with Etsy in real time to avoid confusion, letting you update listings on either app to take advantage of Etsy's marketplace audience.

If you want to use the Shopify point-of-sale without building a store, the Shopify Starter Plan—formerly Shopify Lite—costs $15 per month and provides product pages, checkout, Inbox, and Linkpop. You might miss the Basic Plan's features, like theme editing and blog posts, but the Starter Plan is a quick way to get direct sales up and running on your mobile website, email campaigns, or social media.

Joanna Penn has discussed the ways she uses Shopify with her WordPress site extensively on her podcast, *The Creative Penn*. She recently spoke with Thomas Umstaddt Jr. of *The Novel Marketing Podcast* about the details of selling and marketing direct. While they primarily cover Shopify and its many integrations, they also compare Payhip, Gumroad, and Kickstarter as options for first-time authors.

YOU WANT TO ADD DIRECT SALES TO YOUR EXISTING WORDPRESS WEBSITE: WOOCOMMERCE

An alternative to creating your store on a separate website, WooCommerce is a standard plugin available for paid WordPress accounts that allows you to process sales on your existing author website. It's open source, which allows for customization but also means you might find bugs or integration problems.

WooCommerce is free to use if you already have a WordPress site, but you won't have Shopify's customer service to support you, and some themes and integrations will have additional fees.

The WordPress Business or Commerce plans that allow these types of plugins cost $25 or $45 per month. WordPress offers more features and customization than most authors will ever need but requires more technical knowledge to manage well.

Ultimately, adding WooCommerce to an existing site gives you fewer setup fees and more control than Etsy but doesn't provide the support and features of Shopify.

If you're looking for a more detailed side-by-side look at the two, Jason Hamilton compared WooCommerce and Shopify for Kindlepreneur in July 2023.

WIX

YOU'RE NOT USING WORDPRESS, BUT YOU'D LIKE TO RUN DIRECT SALES THROUGH YOUR AUTHOR WEBSITE: WIX/SQUARESPACE

Both Wix and Squarespace offer commerce plans that have sales features built into their website designers. Wix is best known for being user-friendly and easy to design, while Squarespace has a reputation for responsible growth and a people-first philosophy.

Wix provides basic e-commerce at their Core Plan level for $27 per month. Business ($32 per month) and Business Elite ($159 per month) plans offer additional features. Building the shop is easy because of drag-and-drop design tools. It connects to payment gateways like PayPal, Stripe, and Square, as well as its own Wix Payments option, with no transaction fees.

Squarespace offers fully integrated e-commerce at a 3 percent transaction fee with its Business Plan for $23 per month, or you can upgrade to a Commerce Plan for either $27 or $49 per month with no transaction fees, depending on whether you require basic or advanced features. The primary difference is that the advanced plan offers features to improve shipping, allow discounts, and sell subscriptions. All three plans allow unlimited products, courses, memberships, and videos on demand. The Commerce plans sync with Square so that you can sell in-person through your website and track sales, inventory, and customers with the same analytics as your online sales. The Commerce plans also allow you to collect and display reviews, sell through Facebook and Instagram, and use advanced merchandising features.

Wix and Squarespace both integrate with drop-shipping companies like Printful and Printify to make fulfillment of some products easier. You may need a third-party service to integrate your book printer. Lulu currently only integrates directly with Woo, Shopify, and Lulu API. However, BookVault now integrates with Wix directly.

Both Wix and Squarespace have email campaign features that allow you to sync your store with your newsletter, making the websites a one-stop shop for most of your customer-facing author business needs.

OTHER OPTIONS TO CONSIDER

If you're not using one of the previously mentioned hosts, check and see if your current website builder has e-commerce features. Moving to direct sales may just be a matter of upgrading your current hosting plan.

For example, GoDaddy has e-commerce features available. Using a managed WordPress with WooCommerce store, GoDaddy claims to have the lowest fees at 2.3 percent plus thirty cents per transaction. The managed website plan starts at $19.99 per month.

E-commerce platforms like Payhip, Gumroad, and Stan Store allow you to build a store without managing a blog or author website. They'll have bigger fees per sale but no monthly cost. Initially developed for digital creators, these options work best for authors with strong social media presences.

Alternatively, social media platforms Facebook, Instagram, and TikTok all have marketplaces. Even the subscription platform Ream has plans to incorporate direct sales stores for its members in the future.

Pro Tip: IngramSpark is about to launch Share & Sell, a program that will provide you with shareable purchase links you can use to send readers directly to IngramSpark from your website, social media, or business cards. Visit https://ingramspark.com/e-commerce-beta-sign-up to participate in the beta release before the program launches in 2024.

Whether you choose to manage your own merchandise or make use of on-demand services, creating your own store is the next logical step for authors who don't want to depend on retailers. As Fleetwood Mac sings, "Open up. Everything's waiting for you." ∎

Jenn Lessmann

Jenn Lessmann

Jenn Lessmann is the author of Unmagical: a Witchy Mystery and three stories on Kindle Vella. A former barista, stage manager, and high school English teacher with advanced degrees from impressive colleges, she continues to drink excessive amounts of caffeine, stay up later than is absolutely necessary, and read three or four books at a time. Jenn is currently studying witchcraft and the craft of writing, and giggling internally whenever they intersect. She writes snarky paranormal fantasy for new adults whenever her dog will allow it.

Demystifying BookFunnel

HOW AUTHORS CAN MAKE THE MOST OF THE E-BOOK DISTRIBUTION SERVICE

For many authors, helping readers download e-books purchased directly onto their preferred reading app eats away from valuable writing and marketing time. With so many responsibilities in running a writing business, tech support is a low priority. That's where a tool like BookFunnel (http://www.bookfunnel.com) comes in. It's a digital book delivery service that can help authors with the trickiest parts of e-book fulfillment.

But BookFunnel isn't just a tool for side-loading e-books onto devices. The service offers many additional features to help authors with book distribution and marketing. Here's an in-depth look at BookFunnel and some features authors may not be aware of.

BOOKFUNNEL BASICS

BookFunnel was founded in 2015, and it helps authors deliver their books to readers with ease. Whether they're distributing an ARC, a reader magnet, or bonus content such as a short story or deleted chapter, authors remain in control of the delivery settings through the site.

According to the BookFunnel website, key elements of all BookFunnel services include:

- Reader privacy and no ads
- Link security and watermarking to protect uploaded media
- GDPR compliance
- Unlimited book uploads
- Custom landing pages

The result is a secure distribution channel that enables authors to share their work seamlessly while also maintaining control over the process, reaching readers, and protecting their work.

PRICING

BookFunnel currently has three paid plan tiers for authors. They do not offer a free trial or a demo; the platform's entry-level plan is $20 per year and allows users to take advantage of its core features. Refer to the table below for a high-level overview of each plan.

First-Time Author Plan ($20 per year)	Mid-List Author Plan ($100 per year or $8 per month)	Bestseller Plan ($250 per year or $20 per month)
Only 1 pen name	Up to 2 pen names	Up to 3 pen names
Up to 500 reader downloads per month	Up to 5,000 reader downloads per month	Unlimited reader downloads

Visit the BookFunnel website for more information and a detailed table outlining the features available in each plan.

BOOKFUNNEL FEATURES AVAILABLE ON ALL PLANS

Although not an exhaustive list, authors at all levels will likely find the following BookFunnel features helpful in their book distribution and marketing.

Author Swaps

The Author Swap feature enables authors to find other authors in their genre and share each other's BookFunnel links, allowing readers to download their book in exchange for their email address. Once agreed, each author shares the other's book to their newsletter, driving email signups and building both authors' lists.

Group Promos

Instead of doing a one-to-one author swap, authors can participate in a group promo, which is a similar setup but involves multiple authors at once. A group promo runs for a limited period, during which all participating authors send their readers to a dedicated landing page with all the books featured. Readers can then download the books they are interested in.

Any BookFunnel author can create a Group Promo by logging into their dashboard and clicking the "Group Promos" button on the left-hand navigation of the home screen.

A

screenshot of the Science Fiction & Fantasy Promo board on the BookFunnel dashboard November 20, 2023.

Read Now Pages

BookFunnel's Read Now feature allows readers to read books in the cloud instead of side-loading the books onto their device. This is a helpful option to let readers know about in case they don't want to or cannot side-load books onto a reading app. Read Now pages are accessible from any BookFunnel landing page by clicking the words "Start reading in your browser" underneath the download button.

Easy Ebook Samples

With Easy Ebook Samples, authors embed samples of their e-book on their BookFunnel landing pages so that readers can read the sample directly in the browser. Authors can also add various retailer links to the page, reminiscent of Draft2Digital's Universal Book Links feature. When the reader is ready to buy, they can do so from the retailer links on the page.

Pro Tip: The BookFunnel App launched in 2015 for Android and in 2020 for iOS. The app can send books directly to readers' preferred reading app. It also allows readers to read books directly in the app, and it has an audiobook player for audiobooks delivered through the service.

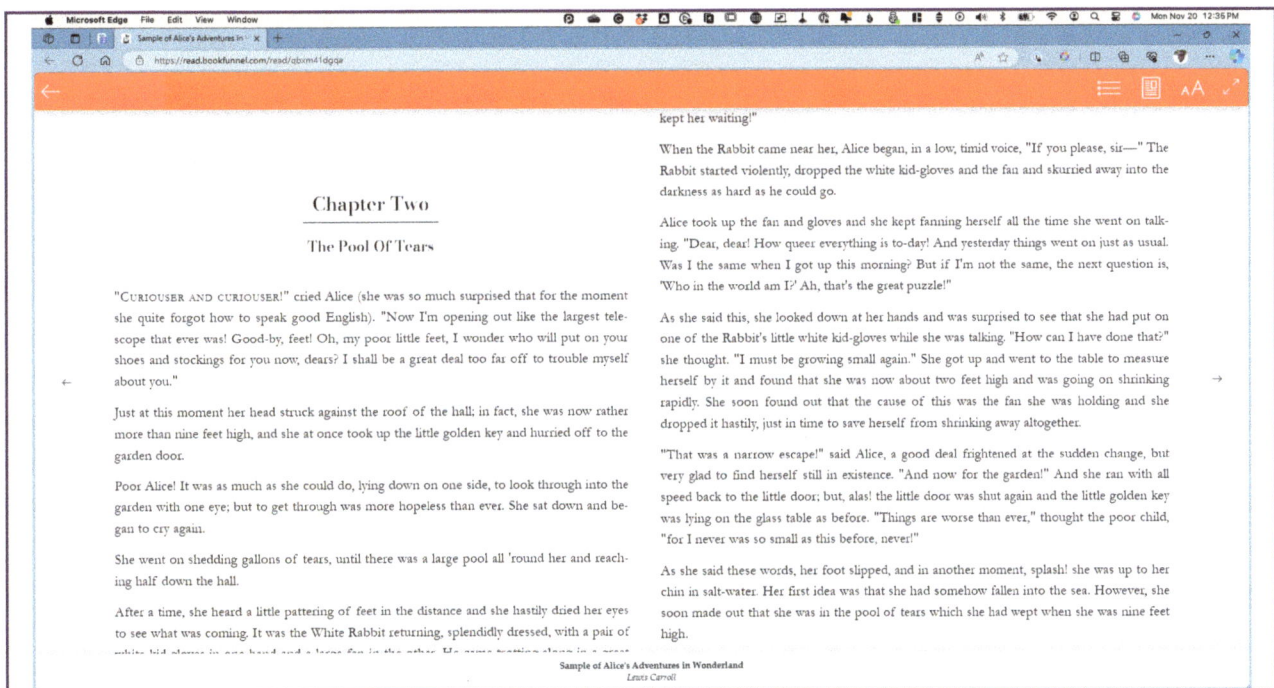

Readers can page through the book in the browser, like this sample of Alice in Wonderland, *and they can adjust reading settings as they would in a traditional e-book reading app.*

An example sales page where readers can buy the book or read the sample.

FEATURES ON THE MID-LIST AUTHOR PLAN (AND ABOVE)

Authors who are willing to spend more money for the Mid-List Plan will benefit from the following additional features to assist in their book delivery and marketing.

Audiobook Delivery

The Mid-List Plan and above allow authors to deliver "short audio" to readers, which BookFunnel defines as up to 120 minutes for spoken word content. Examples of short audio could include audiobook samples, short story readings, behind-the-scenes commentary read by the author, or other creative ideas.

BookFunnel also offers full audiobook delivery, currently in beta. Readers can listen to the audiobook in the BookFunnel app or download the MP3s to their computer if the author allows it. According to BookFunnel, the audiobook delivery feature will eventually be an add-on service for an additional yearly fee.

Certified Mail

Authors who want to deliver ARCs to their "street teams" of early reviewers can use the Certified Mail feature to send each reader a unique secure BookFunnel link that can't be shared with anyone else. The e-book file is watermarked for additional security.

Authors can write the body of the email that goes out with the book, as well as an automated reminder email that nudges readers to leave reviews. The author will receive a summary email after the campaign closes that details which reviewers downloaded the book.

Print Codes

Authors who attend in-person events can take advantage of BookFunnel's Print Codes feature, which are codes allowing for a free e-book or audiobook download. These codes are useful to add to card stock, bookmarks, or any printed materials an author might hand out at an event.

Once print codes are redeemed, they cannot be used again. Authors can generate up to 500 print codes per month.

Pro Tip: Check the BookFunnel Author Knowledge Base (https://authors.bookfunnel.com) for detailed tutorials and tips on using BookFunnel's features.

Direct Integration with Other Services

Authors can integrate BookFunnel with the following services to maximize the selling and delivery process.

Mailing List Providers: BookFunnel integrates with common mailing list providers such as ConvertKit and Mailerlite and enables authors to send BookFunnel links to their existing subscribers as well as collect new email subscribers when they download the author's books.

Direct Sales Providers: Platforms such as Gumroad and Payhip allow authors to enable BookFunnel delivery for readers directly at the point of sale. They'll receive an email with their link when the purchase is complete.

Zapier: Zapier opens up many possibilities since Zapier connects dozens of services. For more information on Zapier, read the October 2023 feature on the platform by *Indie Author Magazine* co-founder Chelle Honiker at https://indieauthormagazine.com/zippier-with-zapier.

Pro Tip: If you sell books direct, sell bundles and fulfill them with BookFunnel using their direct sales integration.

FINAL WORDS

If you haven't explored BookFunnel and its array of features beyond simple book file distribution, it may be worth it in order to maximize your BookFunnel subscription. BookFunnel has become an indispensable tool for indie authors and for readers, and its plethora of features will help you take your marketing to the next level.

Happy BookFunneling! ■

Michael La Ronn

Michael La Ronn

Michael La Ronn has published over 80 science fiction & fantasy books and self-help books for writers. He built a writing career publishing 10-12 books per year while raising a family, working a full-time job, and even attending law school classes in the evenings. He is also the Outreach Manager at the Alliance of Independent Authors, a nonprofit organization for self-published writers. Visit his fiction website at www.michaellaronn.com and his resources for writers at www.authorlevelup.com.

From the Stacks

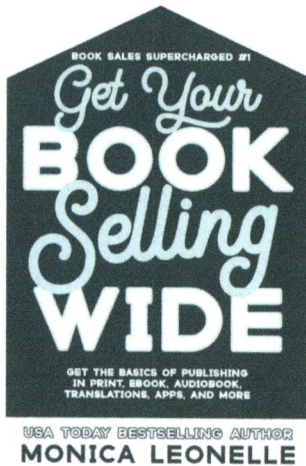

Get Your Book Selling Wide

https://theworldneedsyourbook.com/shop/product/get-your-book-selling-wide

Get Your Book Selling Wide by Monica Leonelle aims to address the fear of putting your eggs into one basket by encouraging distribution of ebooks across multiple platforms—and how to do it. The book also covers strategies for distributing audiobooks, translations, and foreign rights, all with the same idea: that having the maximum reach and finding the most readers is the best strategy for a fruitful indie author career. Leonelle's book addresses the issues around exclusivity, and how your book launch process differs when pushing to other platforms.

TinyURL

https://tinyurl.com/app

TinyURL is a tool that shortens the length of URLs, making them easier to share, trackable, and more visually appealing. Reaching readers is one of the greatest struggles an author can have. Removing every barrier between author and reader should be at the forefront of an author's marketing strategy. This includes long strings of text that clog the reader's email. Using TinyURL, you will add credibility through a professional-looking link and give more insight into your audience through specific link-tracking capabilities.

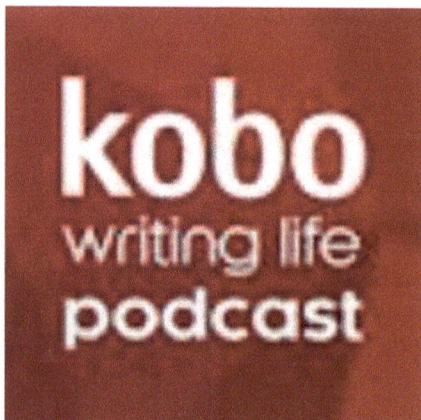

Kobo Writing Life

https://kobowritinglife.libsyn.com

Kobo Writing Life Podcast is run by the distribution platform Kobo and offers insights into the self-publishing industry by bringing on bestselling authors and industry experts for interviews. KWL's recent guests include John Gaspard on the topic of movies and what authors can learn from them, and the realities of indie publishing and writing Romance with J. Sterling. Kobo is but one distributor who would be considered part of the "wide" distribution stack, meaning to publish e-books, you are not required to be exclusive to that platform.

THE NUANCE THAT'S SOMETIMES LOST IN THE TRADITIONAL OR INDIE DEBATE

Authors, take your corners! It's the indie-versus-trad knock-out round. In the indie corner are the authors with complete creative control, slaves to no master, with the freedom to chart their own course. In the trad corner are the authors with editorial and marketing support, and the all-important ingredient of credibility. Winner takes the royalties!

But is it really that clear-cut?

The traditional-versus-indie publishing debate often oversimplifies the realities faced by authors in both realms. The decision to publish traditionally or independently is nuanced and depends on an author's goals, preferences, and the specific project at hand. So how does an author decide which path to pursue? Five authors with unique publishing backgrounds shared the factors they considered when making the choice for their own books, as well as the way the decisions have shaped their experiences in the author world.

SHARED REALITIES

Indie authors are well acquainted with the demands of marketing their own work. From building an online presence to managing promotional efforts, indie authors actively engage in the marketing process. But contrary to the perception that traditional publishers handle all marketing, many traditionally published authors actively participate in promoting their books as well, and authors are increasingly expected to leverage their platforms and engage with readers. Check out BookBub's February 2017 article, "How Traditionally Published Authors Market Their Books," for insights into this.

Marketing isn't the only responsibility shared by traditional and indie authors. Traditional publishing, indie publishing, and the various hybrid versions of the two can be more similar than many realize in several respects. In others, the pros and cons of each publishing route tend to balance out.

Building and maintaining an author platform is crucial for many indie authors. This includes managing social media accounts, cultivating a mailing list, and establishing a personal brand. Traditional publishers also value authors with strong platforms, and some even ask for evidence of such at the submission stage. A sizable and engaged audience enhances an author's appeal to publishers and contributes to a book's success.

One of the primary attractions of self-publishing is the autonomy it offers. Indie authors maintain control over cover design, release schedules, and content without navigating the approval process of a traditional publisher. While traditional publishing provides a team of professionals to guide the process, authors may need to relinquish some creative control. This trade-off is a significant factor for those valuing editorial support and a collaborative publishing experience and is the reason some traditionally published authors explore self-publishing for specific projects or genres.

Self-published authors often leverage online platforms for distribution, with a focus on e-books and print-on-demand services. Building visibility requires strategic marketing efforts. Meanwhile, traditional publishing provides access to established distribution networks, increasing the likelihood of bookstore placement. Publishers also contribute to marketing efforts, enhancing a book's visibility.

The indie publishing process is known for its agility, allowing authors to release books more quickly. This can be advantageous for timely topics or series releases. Traditional publishing, while offering extensive support, follows a longer timeline. Authors might opt for this route for the credibility associated with a traditional imprint and the comprehensive publishing process.

To better understand the ways these publishing paths can affect authors' careers, five authors—including an indie author, a traditionally published author, and a hybrid author—shared how and why they chose to pursue their respective publishing methods.

THE INDIE AUTHOR: JACQUELINE HAYLEY

"I grew up reading Mills & Boon, and I submitted my first book to Harlequin and Entangled [publishing companies], and waited … But I wanted to get my story out into the world! I'm impatient and like to do things my own way, so as soon as I made the decision to self-publish, I didn't look back.

"To be fair, I have experience and skills—my background is in graphic design and digital marketing—that make self-publishing less daunting than it may be to others.

"As an indie author, I work for myself, to my own deadlines. This could be a con for others, but for me it's a definite pro. I also love having complete creative control. I can advertise using Facebook and Amazon ads, and know the exact impact it's having on my books. Being able to see the KDP dashboard—which I monitor daily—allows me to make informed marketing decisions.

"On the flip side, you have to be self-motivated, and willing to invest time into the indie author community. There is no guaranteed income like there is with a royalty check, and it's harder/time intensive to get self-published books into bookstores/libraries."

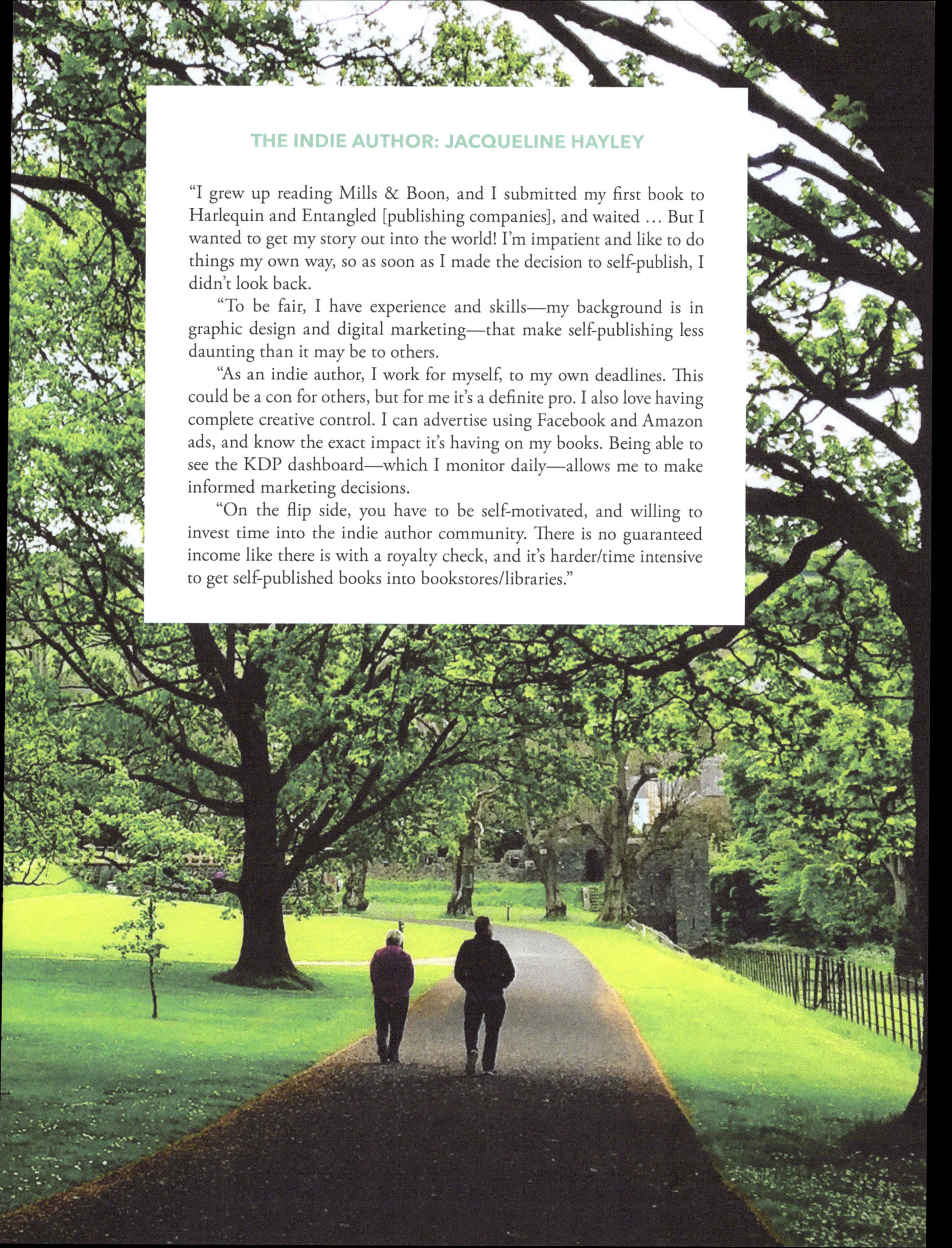

THE TRADITIONALLY PUBLISHED AUTHOR: CASSIE LAELYN

"I set out to be trad published because I wanted to see my book in a bookstore. I signed a contract, worked with a lovely editor and team, and published my book. While I enjoyed the experience and worked with a great editor who has helped me grow as an author, the publisher didn't have the reach/marketing team to push my book onto the shelves of physical stores.

"When the opportunity to contribute to a self-published anthology came along, I took it, wanting to explore another method of publishing. I enjoyed the freedom of designing covers and the publishing timeframe, but I also didn't work so well at setting my own deadlines especially when it came to clashes with my family and high needs child. (This resulted in a lot of personal growth and understanding my Clifton Strengths.)

"I like structure and 'rules' and enjoy trad publishing because it's a systematic plan where I know what to expect. But I don't have control over many aspects and a lot of it is at the mercy of the publisher. Whereas self publishing has so much autonomy that I sometimes get overwhelmed with the sheer amount of steps to navigate."

THE HYBRID AUTHOR: CLARE CONNELLY

"When I chose to publish traditionally, it was never with the intention of pursuing this instead of my self-publishing career, but always as an adjunct. As my indie career grew and the income derived from it became increasingly important to our family, I felt a desire to future-proof that income as much as possible.

"As a lover of category romance, writing for Mills & Boon is something I aspired to for as long as I've been writing—and reading—romance. I'm keen to learn as much as I can as a writer, and as the market leader in category romance, I knew that having the opportunity to work with an experienced editor at Mills & Boon was an opportunity I couldn't turn down.

"There have been some years where juggling traditional and indie publishing has been a bit of a head spin. In 2019, I wrote ten books for Mills & Boon and released at least five self-published titles. The demands of writing that many novels, and writing them well, plus going through the revision and editorial process, meant I was working incredibly long days.

"More than just the writing of these books was the added requirement on the self-publishing side to manage my business, by implementing strategies for diversification and growth, marketing and speaking opportunities, etc. There were definitely times when I couldn't see the forest for the trees. I try really hard not to over-commit myself now, and take a holistic view of my work schedule."

THE INDIE AUTHOR WHO SAID NO TO A PUBLISHER: MICHELLE MONTEBELLO

"I was approached by a major publisher asking to see my current manuscript. I was excited that they'd reached out, but I was also apprehensive because the book was only days away from being independently published. It had been edited several times, had a great cover, all my marketing was in place, and my readers were hungry for it.

"Still, I sent the manuscript to the publisher. It was four months before I heard back from them. They advised me that the ending was fantastic, but the whole first half would have to be rewritten. While I appreciated their feedback, I didn't entirely agree. I decided to go ahead with self-publishing. This book went on to win two awards and drew interest from Voltage Pictures.

"There were several reasons why I decided not to progress to a contract with the publisher. As an indie author, I enjoy complete creative and marketing control of my work. I don't sign the rights to my books away, can put them on sale when I like, and I retain all of my royalties."

THE INDIE AUTHOR WHO SAID YES TO A PUBLISHER: RAE CAERNS

"I always wanted to be traditionally published, but after I wrote my first book and received no interest from any publishers, I made the decision to indie publish. I spent ten months learning the business of self-publishing before I released my book. Then I got lucky. A major newspaper reviewed the book, and that drew the interest of other reviewers, which, in turn, led to wider promotion. The book did pretty well, and it was picked up by Bolinda Publishing as an audiobook.

"In July 2021, I was shortlisted for the Ned Kelly Awards, Australia's oldest and most prestigious awards honoring published Crime Fiction. I didn't win but was inundated with interest. I got an agent and we decided that Harper-Collins was the best fit. Not long after, I signed a two-book deal with them.

"Distribution was the driving force in this decision as I'm under no illusion about the amount of work that goes into marketing and other aspects of the business of publishing. I am happy to hand off the jobs I know I'm not great at to a team of experts I don't have to source. I appreciate and enjoy the team aspects of trad publishing."

***

As the boundaries between traditional and indie publishing blur, authors are presented with a spectrum of possibilities. But the paths are not necessarily mutually exclusive, nor is one inherently better than the other when considering a variety of factors; instead, they can complement each other in a way that aligns with an author's specific goals and aspirations. Whether forging ahead as an indie author, embracing traditional publishing, or navigating the middle ground, authors now have the agency to craft a publishing journey that best serves their unique vision and objectives. ■

Tanya Nellestein

Tanya Nellestein

Tanya Nellestein is an avid reader, experience enthusiast, outstanding car vocalist, and Queen of fancy dress. In her spare time she is also a bestselling and award-winning author and journalist with a penchant for bloodthirsty battles and steamy romance. From Vikings to present day, Tanya writes page-turning, gut-churning stories with a romantic angle that always includes good sex and a happily ever after - eventually. Her debut novel, The Valkyrie's Viking recently hit Amazon's best seller list and her sixth novel, This Side of Fate, was the 2022 winner of the Romance Writers of Australia Sapphire Award for Best Unpublished Romance Manuscript. In 2021, Tanya won the Romance Writers of Australia Romance in Media Award. Tanya lives on the outskirts of Sydney, Australia amidst a cavalcade of never ending disasters, both natural and those of her own making.

Idioms, Explained

EXPLORING THE HISTORY BEHIND THREE COMMON ENGLISH SAYINGS

As writers, we love to play with words. We twirl them around on our tongues and pop them out in various ways. Sometimes we cajole; other times we inspire or inform. We create jokes to entertain or puns that bring on groans.

Occasionally, we use phrases we learned as children, even though we might be uncertain about their meanings or origins. Often, the phrases were first used centuries or even millennia ago. These idioms frequently contain accepted truisms that have survived through the ages. But understanding their meaning, and when they became commonplace, is essential to creating fiction that can keep your readers immersed. In part one of this ongoing series, we're exploring the origins of a few recognizable idioms you may be tempted to use in your writing. Whether you want to ensure your creative turn of phrase truly means what you intend or your historical novel's dialogue is keeping with the times, the list below is a great lesson in what many everyday English sayings actually mean.

'ONCE IN A BLUE MOON'

Example: The woman, doubtful that her husband will clean the garage as promised, scornfully notes, "That will happen only once in a blue moon."

Often used to show a rare occurrence, the phrase "once in a blue moon" is sometimes misleading as a true "blue moon," or a full moon that occurs twice in the same month, will happen about every two and a half years. The moon itself rarely appears blue; that only happens when atmospheric conditions are just right.

"Blue moon" has been a popular phrase in music across generations, starting with Ella Fitzgerald singing the song "Blue Moon" in the 1930s. The popularly attributed authors, Richard Rodgers and Lorenz Milton Hart, were sued for not being the original composers of the song, and they eventually settled with the original author so they could use the music.

Since then, several artists have recorded their versions of the song, including Elvis, Dylan, and Sinatra, along with country singers Roseanne Cash and Toby Keith. Each put their personal touch on the phrase, giving it either a rare or lonely connotation.

'ALL THAT GLITTERS IS NOT GOLD'

Example: The girl quickly learns that all that glitters is not gold when she finds out that her handsome boyfriend is cheating on her.

Meaning that not everything is truly as wonderful as it may appear on the surface, this phrase shows up in French medieval literature, *The Canterbury Tales*, and eventually Shakespeare's play *The Merchant of Venice*, where he used the word "glister" instead of the now popular word "glitter."

People sometimes used the phrase literally in nineteenth-century searches for the precious metal when prospectors or miners were misdirected by finding mica, or "fool's gold." Also, in the mid-nineteenth century, writers Theodore Heaton and Welford Vawn used the phrase for the title of a song that became popular then.

In the late twentieth century, the phrase was turned around and used by the rock band Led Zeppelin in their song "Stairway to Heaven," still covered today, when they say "All that glitters is gold." Even more recently than that, the movie *Fool's Gold* starring Kate Hudson and Matthew McConaughey, was released in 2008.

'FACE THE MUSIC'

Example: The student, who was caught cheating on his exam, had to face the music and accept a failing grade on the test.

To "face the music" is to own up to one's actions by addressing the consequences. Although the origins of this phrase are murky, we find it as an American phrase in the nineteenth century in a military context, according to Grammarist. A soldier who had not followed orders could be forced to leave his unit by walking past his comrades to a drumbeat. Other references describe actors who receive their first critiques after a live performance by looking at the orchestra pit they face before seeing the audience.

In the 1930s, Irving Berlin used the phrase "Let's face the music and dance" in a song in the movie *Follow the Fleet* with Fred Astaire and Ginger Rogers. The 1980s saw a TV show of that same name, while more recently, The New Kids on the Block released an album titled *Face the Music*.

Remember, in writing, as in life, there can be too much of a good thing. When overused, idioms can lose their punch—and possibly your reader. Just as you moderate slang and your own overused phrases, do the same with idioms. Then they can be appreciated for the unique zing they bring to your story.

What idioms, phrases, or sayings should we explore next? Email us at feedback@indieauthormagazine.com! ■

Sharon Kay Dooley

Sharon Kay Dooley

"Sharon Kay Dooley is a semi-retired Registered Nurse who has been a writer since her high school days. Sharon loves word games, Wordle, and puzzles. She has always been a reader and reads everything except horror and most Sci-fi. Currently, she is writing a series of children's books and an environmentally based cozy mystery series.

Since she lives in MD near the nation's capital, she keeps an eye on politics and the Washington Football Team-The Commanders. She includes among her special favorites her two children, and her grandchildren. Other likes are cooking, drinking excellent coffee, eating chocolate desserts, and walks with her rescue dog."

Hone Your Home Writing Setup

ERGONOMIC WORKSPACES PROTECT YOUR HEALTH AND YOUR CAREER'S LONGEVITY

As authors, we navigate the landscape of our imagination, but at the helm of our adventures is an often-unacknowledged force: the ergonomics of our writing space. Even if it doesn't seem to matter much in the short-term, the setup we choose can shape the contours of our literary endeavors over time. Developing habits to promote personal productivity and prevent repetitive work damage leads to better health and well-being, whatever your chosen workspace.

COZY WRITING SPOT

Standard desk ergonomics should always apply to your writing spot, be it a home office, a tidy corner in your home, or a café table. My writing place is a home office with an L-shaped desk that has a pull-out shelf to hold my keyboard. I keep a ninety-degree elbow angle with my keyboard and mouse as I work. My chair keeps my feet on the floor and my body supported. A good pair of investments are a lumbar support pillow for the back and a coccyx cushion to help with spine alignment. I also have my monitor raised to eye level to help keep my back straight.

I use a mechanical keyboard with an ergonomic mouse when I write, and when I am not typing, I take my hands from the keyboard and rest my elbow on my armrests to prevent carpal tunnel and keep pressure off my wrists. Since I leave my hand on my mouse most of the time, I prefer a wrist rest paired with my device. If you are a writer who tends to leave your hands on the keyboard as you think, you might benefit from a wrist rest—though use it sparingly.

Some authors prefer to write in a café or in other locations away from home. Even if you don't have total control of the environment where you work, there are small steps you can take to still protect your well-being as you write. When I write at my local café, I bring a foldable laptop riser to elevate my laptop's screen to eye level and bring a separate keyboard so I can find a good typing height. It is never perfect, but I find the change of scene to be beneficial, especially when I'm drafting a new story or composing poetry.

I do not write on a couch, the floor, or a bed, but many writers do. It can be difficult to find an ergonomic position in such places; however, a lap desk that elevates your writing machine from your lap to slightly above waist level could be of use in these circumstances.

Pro Tip: A mechanical keyboard can improve your accuracy and typing speed thanks to the comfortable feel of the key travel. The clicking sound it produces also may help you get into the writing zone faster.

MOTION IN PROSE

Most able-bodied adults should aim to walk at least ten thousand steps per day, according to the Centers for Disease Control and Prevention. As writers, we typically remain seated at our desks as we work. While many of us can incorporate a walk once a day, either at lunch or around dinner time, developing a habit of additional steps as you write can lead to better health. Using a standing desk can get you on your feet for part of the day and allow you to shift back to the seated position as needed. You can also develop a set of habits that allow you to get up from your desk regularly and move through your home. The point is to shift and change your position to help your body combat repetitive movement and avoid staying in the same place for too long.

One way to build a habit of movement into your day is to use the Pomodoro Technique. Set a timer to write for twenty-five minutes, then take a brief break to stand and move around before returning to your desk. These breaks are a great time to walk through your home to get a bottle of water or simply refresh your vision. A stroll away from your screen also helps to combat eye strain. It can refresh your mental clarity and return you to your story with a new vision.

WRITE GEAR, BOOST CRAFT

Creating a healthy writing environment doesn't have to mean a massive redesign; even just incorporating a few small tools to your toolkit can help protect your physical well-being. Over the years, I've added a few items to my writing space to help make my life easier.

Blue-light blocking glasses: Your computer screen emits a blue light, which can cause eyestrain. Some writers put a screen filter on their monitor or wear filtered glasses. Some computers and tablets allow you to shut off blue light altogether. Eye drops are another good way to keep headaches at bay.

Analog bullet journal: One way I get my eyes off screen is to track my tasks via a paper bullet journal. I have mine resting on an artist's easel, so I can glance at my journal without bending over my desk.

Laptop riser: When writing with your laptop, use a regular keyboard instead of the built-in keyboard for long-term writing. A laptop riser will bring your screen to the proper eye level as you work. ■

Wendy Van Camp

Wendy Van Camp

Wendy Van Camp is the Poet Laureate for the City of Anaheim, California. Her work is influenced by cutting edge technology, astronomy, and daydreams. A graduate of the Ad Astra Speculative Fiction Workshop, Wendy is a nominated finalist for the Elgin Award, for the Pushcart Prize, and for a Dwarf Stars Award. Her poems, stories, and articles have appeared in: "Starlight Scifaiku Review", "The Junction", "Quantum Visions", and other literary journals. She is the poet and illustrator of "The Planets: a scifaiku poetry collection" and editor of the annual anthology "Eccentric Orbits: An Anthology of Science Fiction Poetry". Find her at https://wendyvancamp.com

Overcoming Defeat

There are many people who don't make it in this industry. Many, if not most, fall by the wayside because they give up, not because they cannot succeed. Yes, I made it, but that is only because I refused to be beaten as I climbed the mountain.

When I published my first book, it was poorly edited, had a terrible cover I'd bought for $20, and contained at least a thousand words of unnecessary fluff. Consequently, the first review on Amazon.com was a one-star howler, and that was enough to bury the book. No one bought it. I couldn't even give it away.

That same book spent a good portion of last year in the number one spot for its genre on Amazon.com. I rewrote chunks of it. I changed the cover and spent some money. The version readers get now is essentially the same story except the manuscript is slicker, error-free, and looks like a professionally produced book.

The point I want you to take away is that if you have published and you are yet to see success, you will not get there if you allow the journey to beat you. It would have been very easy for me to accept defeat and believe I didn't have what it took to be a commercially successful writer.

A friend of mine wrote fifty—yes, fifty—books before she found the success her words deserved. Her journey serves as a rather extreme example of refusing to be beaten, but there are very few examples of authors, especially indies, who achieve worthwhile sales with their first book or even their first few books.

In fact, if you were to take a sample of the indie authors out there making seven figures a year, I believe you would learn that most had ten books or more published and a couple of years in the game before the money started to come their way.

But what if you have been at this for a decade and still cannot get your books to sell? You may question whether the barrier to success is your ability to write, and it's possible you are right. However, my experience has been that for most writers, the obstacle lies outside the words inside the book.

This should be received as good news.

Covers, blurbs, and even marketing and advertising are areas where you can make easy changes or hire someone to make them for you. Advice is available for free—when you seek it, just make sure you get it from unbiased sources. This may seem obvious, yet it is easier, not to mention more comforting, to get advice from those people around us who will tell us what we want to hear.

This happens all too often with our manuscripts—the people reading them are too close to us to give the feedback we need to hear. But if you look for beta readers who will give honest feedback, you will find them. Additionally, if your writing lacks a certain punch or flow, there are craft books to help you, developmental editors you can hire, and the good old expedient of practice.

Don't give up because you are yet to see success. Analyze where you need to improve, and learn the skills, marketing, writing, or otherwise, that will make your books sell. ■

Steve Higgs

Steve Higgs

High school Valedictorian enlists in the Marine Corps under a guaranteed tank contract. An inauspicious start that was quickly superseded by excelling in language study.

BOOK COVER AUCTIONS

FIND YOUR NEXT COVER

BUY DIRECT FROM DESIGNERS →

ALL GENRES & STYLES →

AUCTIONS & BUY IT NOW →

EASY-TO-USE PLATFORM →

DESIGNERS: CREATE YOUR OWN ETSY-LIKE SHOP, COMPLETE WITH E-COMMERCE & AUCTION FEATURES!

BOOKCOVERAUCTIONS.COM

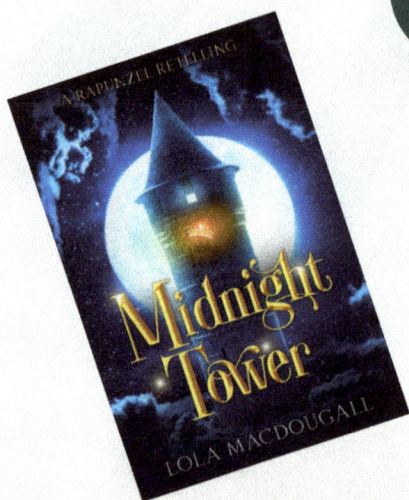

A RAPUNZEL RETELLING

Midnight Tower

LOLA MACDOUGALL

LAUNCHING SOON